THEN AND THERE SERIES
GENERAL EDITOR
MARJORIE REEVES M.A. PH.D.

The Huguenots

ALISON GRANT, B.A.
RONALD MAYO
Docteur de l'Université de Lille (Lettres)

LONGMAN

LONGMAN GROUP LIMITED
London

Associated companies, branches and representatives
throughout the world

© *Longman Group Ltd* 1973

First published 1973

ISBN 0 582 20527 1

Printed by Singapore Offset Printing (Pte.) Ltd.

Contents

To the Reader

You must all have known at some time what it feels like to be in a *minority*, that is, one of a small group, outnumbered and outvoted; by contrast, how safe and easy it is to be in the *majority*, on the winning side. Because the majority is always bigger, it is sometimes tempted to taunt or bully those on the other side and to do something violent and cruel. The ring-leaders know they have support, and unless they are stopped may inflict real suffering. The Huguenots of France in the sixteenth and seventeenth centuries were a minority, different, because of their Protestant religion, from the Catholic majority. The attack on them was not stopped but encouraged by the French government and Church, and so became one of the most terrible *persecutions** of modern times. Those who could escape fled to other countries where their difficulties were once again those of a minority – foreign immigrants.

This story of the Huguenots is written to show you the evils of persecution. We still have problems of minorities and immigrant communities in the twentieth century, but as public opinion can influence governments in their policies, it will be up to you in the future to make sure that all members of the community are allowed to live without fear of persecution.

*Words printed in *italics* are explained in the Glossary at the end,
p. 108.

1 ARTOIS
2 TOURAINE
3 NIVERNAIS
4 BOURBONNAIS
5 LYONNAIS
6 AUNIS
7 ANGOUMOIS
8 LIMOUSIN
9 VENAISSIN

France's ancient provinces

1 Escape

It was dusk on a bitterly cold winter's day when a strange procession set out. First came a man leading a horse with *panniers* at either side, each containing a young child. A girl of nine was riding on the horse's back, while two older boys and a young woman followed on foot. Another man brought up the rear. Soon it became dark, but a six-mile journey lay ahead of the travellers, and the roads were flooded and almost impassable after recent heavy rain. However, the party did not propose to keep to the roads. Here is an account of the journey:

> We *traversed* meadows which were become *quagmires*, or went through *vineyards* whose borders were very high, and the ground so soft we could not advance a step without sinking almost to the calves of our legs. We frequently trod the brinks of precipices, the frightful depths of which we had then no conception of, brinks which in the daytime we should have carefully avoided, and which nothing but the hand of a gracious God could have guided us safely through, in the midst of darkness and ignorance.

Who were these people and where were they going so secretly? The leader of the party was Jean (or in English, John) Migault, a widower in his early forties. The young woman was his eldest daughter, Anne, and the children her younger brothers and sisters. Olivier aged four, and seven-year-old Elisabeth were in the panniers; the little girl on the horse's back was called Marie; the boys walking behind were Louis and Pierre, thirteen and eleven. Jean Dillot, a faithful friend of the family accompanied the party, which was

Refugee family

making its way to Pampin, an estate on the coast a few miles from the great seaport of La Rochelle on the Atlantic coast of France. It was the 16th of January in the year 1688.

When at last the travellers arrived, they went to a small house near the *château* of Pampin, a few yards from a desolate stretch of seashore. Many other refugee families had gathered on the beach, but Migault took his weary children into the house for shelter. Suddenly loud cries were heard and a man ran into the house calling out, 'The guards are on the beach. Save yourselves!' Panic seized some of those who heard, and they fled into the darkness and the wet fields outside. Migault could scarcely hope to escape with all the children, but fortunately the alarm was a false one, and they settled down again to wait. A few minutes later news came that a boat had arrived. Everyone rushed out, but many lost their way in the darkness and confusion, and Migault and his family found themselves in a vineyard a hundred yards from the sea. Someone guided them to the beach, but they arrived just as the boat, with thirty-five people on board, was being rowed off 7 to the English sailing ship which lay at anchor in deep water some distance away. The sailors promised to return.

Jean Migault later wrote the story of his experiences. This is how he described his feelings at the sight of the departing boat: 'We were reduced to the necessity of waiting until the return of the sailors which was not before six o'clock. I need not detail all our sufferings, during this long interval, arising from cold, *fatigue* and anxiety of mind.' Determined not to be left a second time, Migault and his family sat down on a rock close to where the boat had put ashore. But they were again unlucky, for it entered a creek 150 yards away, and in the rush to get to it the young children were once again left behind. Again the sailors said they would return, but they could not keep their promise, for day was dawning and two guard boats were seen, patrolling a little way out to sea. Fear seized those left on the shore, for they knew they could be savagely punished if they were captured.

For Migault and his family the situation had become 'very awful', as he wrote. Terrified and exhausted they fled from the beach, the weary horse only just able to carry the younger children. With them came a young woman who had been separated from her mother, not knowing whether she was on board ship or wandering somewhere in the cold wet countryside. The journey back was worse than the one the night before, for no one had had any sleep. The young woman 'had lost her shoes in the mud the preceding night and could scarcely advance a single step. I was unable to render her much assistance,' wrote Migault, 'for my strength was exhausted, and Dillot had to carry two of the children by turns, whose situation was, perhaps, more distressing than this young lady's.'

Fortunately the young woman's mother was found, and the whole party was able to return to her house at La Rochelle, although the next day the children had to be taken to friends outside the town as it was too dangerous to remain there. At Easter they returned again, arousing no suspicion among the holiday crowds. The weather was fine when they set out for Pampin, and this time they embarked safely on the waiting ship and eventually got to Holland.

Refugees embarking

You may be wondering why it was necessary to face such difficulties and dangers, and why the Migaults with thousands of others were leaving their native land. To find the answers it is necessary to go back to the century before Migault was born, and follow the story of the French Protestants—the Huguenots.

2 Early Huguenots

The name Huguenots began to be used for French Protestants more than a hundred years before our story, soon after
1560. At about the same time the picture reproduced
opposite was painted. It shows the Huguenot church, or
temple as it was often called, at Lyons, an important town in
south-east France, and by studying it we can find out more
about the Huguenot religion and the ways in which it
differed from the Catholic faith.

You will notice how plain most people's clothes are in the
picture. Men are dressed in simply cut black suits with wide
white collars and tall hats, while women are wearing homely
dresses of grey. Perhaps you have noticed that these costumes
are like those of English Puritans in Oliver Cromwell's time.
This is because the Puritans had the same ideas as the
Huguenots and rich clothes with lace and ribbons had
no part in their simple godly lives. In a Catholic church, the
priest would be wearing beautifully embroidered robes
called vestments, but the man in the pulpit at Lyons is
wearing the same plain clothes as the others. This was not
only because the Huguenots disapproved of vestments, but
because they did not believe that there should be a priest at
all. Instead they had ministers who served the congregation
but were not set apart from them. Often they were called
pastors, which means shepherds, as they took care of their
flocks.

The Huguenot churches were very plain too, like the one
in the picture. Notice the hard narrow planks that served for
seats—although better-off people had more comfortable ones
which you can see each side of the pulpit. You will not see the

Huguenot family at Lyons

statues, candles and richly carved ornaments which are found in a Catholic church. The Huguenots did not think these things necessary for the worship of God. You will see, too, that this church was round in shape, whereas a Catholic church was usually shaped like a cross with an altar at one end for the celebration of *Mass*, their most sacred service. Catholics believed, as they still do, that the bread and wine used in this service were the body and blood of Jesus, who was really present at the altar. Thus it was natural for the Catholics to rail off the altar and kneel in front of it at Mass. The Huguenots' beliefs were different. They said that Jesus 11 had asked his disciples at the Last Supper to take bread and wine in remembrance of Him, so they often placed the Lord's Table in the centre of the church or in some part where all might gather round it for the *symbolic* meal.

In Catholic churches, men take off their hats in reverence to God, but in the picture the Huguenots have theirs on. They took them off, however, when prayers were being said or the Bible was read. To them the Bible was very important as the only way in which God's will could be made known. Catholics agreed that the Bible was important, but said that people should also 'hear the Church' which for centuries had made rules for people's worship and their lives. Some of these rules had been made by early writers and others by Popes, whom Catholics believe to be the successors to St Peter as head of the Catholic Church. Huguenots would not believe anything unless it was mentioned in the Bible, and as they could find nothing about bishops and Popes, they would not accept these either.

The Huguenots also took off their hats when the name of God was spoken. They must have had a busy time in some sermons! As you will see by the position and size of the pulpit in the picture, preaching was a very important part of their worship. The minister had an hour-glass at his elbow in case he should go on too long, but many of his followers would not have minded, for they enjoyed their services. Here is Jean Migault's description of secret worship when he and his family were in hiding: 'We devoted this Sabbath to prayer, singing and hearing the Word [of God, the Bible]. We divided the service into two parts agreeably to the manner of the French reformed [that is Huguenot] churches, and the young man who was sent to me delivered two admirable sermons. We all felt refreshed and comforted in our souls.' If the worshippers had been discovered, all would have been imprisoned, for by that time the Huguenots were being persecuted, and their temples destroyed. Even when the picture was painted well over a hundred years earlier, there was danger. Have you noticed that there were no windows on the ground floor? This was in case enemies should spy on or even shoot those inside.

It is likely that the picture shows a wedding or a baptism with just a few families present. Someone has even brought the dog. On Sundays, however, the church would be crowded, for Protestant ideas had been spreading rapidly in France since the 1520s soon after Martin Luther had challenged the Catholic religion in Germany. Travellers and traders brought the news to other countries and people listened eagerly, for the Catholic Church was not popular, owing to its great wealth and the bad example set by some churchmen of the time. When Luther was ordered to give up his ideas, he threw the Pope's *bull* or letter on a public bonfire. Soon he had many followers known as Protestants, because their leaders had drawn up a protest and refused to return to the Catholic Church.

The first French Protestants were Lutherans, but soon a new leader appeared whose influence in France became much greater, for he was himself a Frenchman. This was Jean Calvin, born in 1509 in north-eastern France, at Noyon

Jean (John) Calvin

in Picardy. He was a quiet, delicate boy, clever and deeply religious. (It is interesting that both Luther and Calvin were good Catholics at first.) Calvin was training to be a priest when his father had a quarrel with the Church and sent him to study law instead, so he had a well trained mind. Then in 1533 he felt he had been called by God, and joined the Protestants. In the next few years he travelled around France, finding many people ready to listen, even though persecution had already begun. Calvin was forced to hold his meetings in secret, in places such as this cave near Poitou in the west of France. It was half way up a rocky cliff face but in spite of that many followers came to hear him preach, and when he left the district, they carried on his work.

Calvin's cave

Calvin was soon forced to leave France, and after a time he settled in Geneva, a Swiss city which had just overthrown its Catholic bishop. The city was in a dreadful state, with violence, drunkenness and *immorality* very common. Calvin believed in a strict life as well as strict religion, and soon put his ideas into practice. Twelve *elders* were chosen who 'purified' religion and manners under Calvin's direction. Drunkenness and swearing were stopped and people accused of immorality were sent to court for trial. People who did not go to church could be punished too, and dancing and play acting were *banned*, for such pleasures were thought to be wrong. Most of us would find such a society hard to live in, but many people in Geneva were grateful to Calvin for restoring peace and good government. The poor were looked after, hospitals opened, prison conditions improved, and Calvin even took an interest in the town drains. Perhaps his most important work for Geneva was in education, for he encouraged schools and founded a university to which Protestants flocked from many other countries, although, sad to say, non-Protestants were persecuted for their religious beliefs, for few people in those days believed in *toleration*. In spite of this, by the time Calvin died in 1564 Geneva was known as a 'glorious European city' and Calvin's ideas had spread from it, far and wide.

One of those who took Calvin's ideas back to his native France was Philibert Hamelin, who travelled through the country selling Bibles which he had printed himself. Perhaps he had learnt this skill in Geneva where there was more than one printing press. Printing enabled Luther and Calvin to spread their ideas quickly, and Bibles in their own language were very popular among Protestants. Catholics kept to Latin Bibles, and were alarmed at the spread of Protestant publications. Sometimes they ordered these to be burnt in public, but this did not have a great effect as printing presses produced so many copies that they could not all be destroyed.

Hamelin's travels finally brought him to the little town of Saintes in Saintonge, a province on the west coast of France. Here he set up a Protestant church and became its first minister, but he was taken prisoner by order of the bishop,

Early printing works

and in spite of efforts made by his friends, was hanged. Six
humble poor men decided to carry on his work, and they met
each Sunday with other Protestants, taking it in turn to
preach, though none was a minister. Then a little later they
got a *pastor*, and the congregation grew, although not without
difficulties. The minister left, and a third was found, of whom
one of the congregation wrote:

> The poor man was shut up like a prisoner, and very fre-
> quently ate apples and drank water for his dinner; and
> for want of a tablecloth, he very often laid his dinner on a
> shirt, because there were very few rich people who joined

our congregation, and so we had not the means of paying him his salary.

In spite of persecution and poverty, the number of Protestants in the town continued to grow, and soon had its effect on the lives of the people. The same man wrote:

> The Protestant faith had so well prospered in a few years, that already the games, dances, ballads, banquets and *superfluities* of headdress and gildings had almost all ceased. There were no more scandalous words or murders. . . . You would have seen in those days on a Sunday, fellow tradesmen rambling through the fields, groves and other pleasant places, singing in troops, psalms, *canticles* and spiritual songs, reading and instructing one another.

At this happy time, his followers would have agreed that Philibert Hamelin, the founder of their church, had not worked and suffered in vain. Unfortunately the Protestants of Saintes could not long enjoy their psalm-singing rambles, for renewed persecution soon forced them to worship in secret at dead of night – if they lived to do even that.

All over France, but particularly in the south and west, brave men like Hamelin were spreading the new religion, and by 1560 it is thought that there were over one million Huguenots. Catholics were alarmed, which helps to account for persecution becoming more common. Then in 1562 came civil war, which the kings of France could not stop, and sometimes even joined in. Many nobles took sides to further their own ambitions, and they found the easiest way to gain followers was to declare themselves *ardent* Catholics or sincere Protestants. Indeed, some were so. Thus, in the name of Christ who came to bring peace on earth, were fought some of the cruellest campaigns in history – the French Wars of Religion.

3 Wars of Religion

Francis duke of Guise

A bell was ringing in the little town of Vassy in Normandy when Francis, duke of Guise rode past at the head of a troop of soldiers one Sunday morning in the spring of 1562. 'It is calling the Huguenots to their sermon', he was told. 'Huguenots! Huguenots! 'Sdeath I will "huguenotise" them before long!' he swore. Soon afterwards fifty or sixty Huguenots lay dead and another two hundred wounded in a barn where they had gathered to worship on the outskirts of the town. Guise, who had ordered his followers to spare nobody, earned the nickname 'butcher' for these and other atrocities which led to the wars of religion. Less than a year later he was shot in the back by a Huguenot who had trailed him to a lonely wood where he was riding with only a few companions. The assassin was soon captured, and after fiendish tortures, was executed.

Thus the scene was set for the wars of religion. *Massacre*, assassination, torture and execution were as common as sieges and battles. Fierce hatred led to unspeakable brutality on both sides. Guise and others had Huguenots hanged, drowned in sacks, or broken on the wheel. Many pictures and

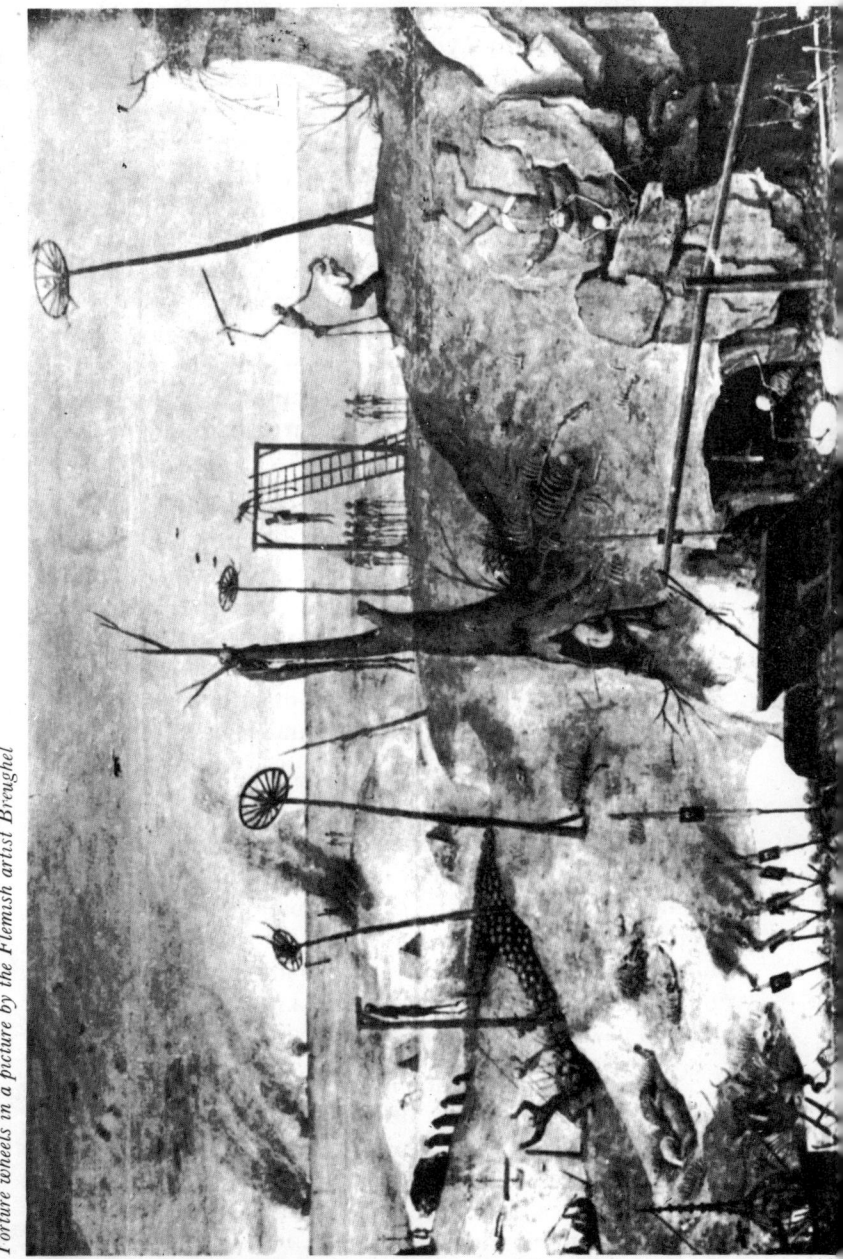

Torture wheels in a picture by the Flemish artist Breughel

prints of the time show the great wheels erected for this purpose outside towns and villages. The victims' limbs were tied to the spokes, to be broken by an iron bar as the wheel slowly revolved. Huguenots themselves could be just as cruel. One leader ordered monasteries and nunneries to be burnt without allowing any of the inmates to escape. They treated priests with the utmost indignity; on one occasion, in Dieppe a number were buried in the ground up to their shoulders, while the Huguenots, playing a vicious game of ninepins, hurled large wooden balls at their heads.

Armies lived on the countryside. Foreign *mercenaries*, particularly the 'Black Troopers' from Germany, swept through France like a thunderbolt, as one writer put it, destroying and plundering. French armies were often as bad, and ordinary people suffered terribly.

> Agriculture was abandoned, multitudes of towns and villages, *pillaged* and burnt, were deserted, and the poor labourers, driven from their houses, *despoiled* of their furniture and cattle, robbed today by one party, tomorrow by another, fled like wild beasts leaving all they had to the mercy of those who were without mercy. Commerce was quite given up; no one was secure of his property or life. Thus the war, undertaken for religion, *annihilated* religion and piety.

The bloodshed, disease and starvation lasted for over thirty years, and it has been estimated that almost a third of the population of France died. Such was the cost of these wars.

Guise's assassin 'informed' his captors that he had been hired by a notable Huguenot leader, Gaspard de Coligny, to murder the duke. The confession, made under torture, was not taken seriously by those who knew Coligny, for his character was generally admired:

> He was remarkable for his prudence and coolness; his manners were *austere*; he always appeared serious and thoughtful. His speech was grave, he was skilled in the Latin tongue and the study of religion; and he grew in people's love, the more they knew of his frankness and devotion to his friends.

Coligny

This praise was written, not by one of Coligny's friends, but by the Pope's ambassador, who had every reason to dislike the Huguenots. Few people, therefore, believed that a man so respected would stoop to plot a murder. But the dead man's son, Henry, now duke of Guise himself, thought differently and swore to be avenged. This bitter enmity was to have terrible consequences.

Coligny bore the title Admiral of France, a high honour, but not much connected with ships at that time. In fact, he shared the command of the Huguenot armies in the wars of religion, with Louis, prince of Condé. After the prince was killed in battle, Coligny remained in sole charge. His skill lay in raising troops and equipping them, rather than in the actual battles. He fought with courage, but did not always win. Yet he never gave up, and his enemies declared he was more dangerous after a defeat than after a victory, for he would quickly re-organise his troops to strike again.

Sixteenth-century battles were part medieval and part modern. Bow and arrow had been replaced by *arquebus* or *musket*. To fire the long-barrelled arquebus, the marksman pulled a trigger. This released the '*match*', a piece of slow burning rope, which fell on some gunpowder in a little 'pan', setting light to the main charge which fired the bullet. Before the arquebusier could pull the trigger, he had to take the cover off the 'pan', adjust the 'match' so that it fell in exactly the right place, and blow on it to make it burn more brightly; a tricky and time-consuming business! Muskets, which were bigger and over twice as powerful, had to be placed on a forked rest.

While reloading, arquebusiers would shelter under the long *pikes* of the men behind them. About one third of the *infantry* consisted of pikemen who, armed with their eighteen-foot weapons, would stand shoulder to shoulder to withstand the shock of a *cavalry* charge. Behind them again were the *halberdiers*, whose weapons being shorter than the pike could be used in hand-to-hand fighting with any knights who broke through.

Knights in armour were still to be seen on the battlefield, but as armour was expensive and heavy, it was less common. Leather coats and boots were beginning to be worn instead. Felt hats with plumes were worn, but many men wore iron caps inside. When a cavalry charge took place, the mounted men would advance in line, draw up their horses, fire their pistols then wheel away, while the next line took their place. Pistols were fired more quickly than the arquebus, having a wheel-lock – a device whereby a metal wheel with a *fluted* surface revolved against a flint which threw sparks down on the powder in the 'pan'. In close fighting, the horsemen would draw their swords.

Artillery was also used in battle, if it arrived in time. It was often too late, for the heaviest cannon weighing well over two tons had to be dragged by twenty-five horses in single file. They often got stuck on bad ground on the way to the battle-field. The biggest cannonballs used in France weighed about thirty-four pounds. Culverins – smaller guns – fired balls weighing two, seven or fifteen pounds, while the smallest guns, called falcons and falconets, had balls of seventeen and fourteen ounces respectively. It took, on average, five minutes to load and fire such weapons, and they were difficult to aim, as the roughly rounded balls often did not fit the badly

Cannon

Musketeer

Halberdier

Pikeman

Sixteenth century soldiers and weapons

made barrels. But at least the noise might scare the enemy, and sometimes real damage was done!

Here is the story of one battle to show you how sixteenth-century wars were fought. It took place at Moncontour in Poitou in October 1569. A great deal depended on choosing a good position, but just before the battle Coligny's German mercenaries laid down their arms, saying they would not fight until they were paid. It took an hour and a half to find the money and settle the trouble, so that the Huguenots were unable to reach favourable ground. All at once the enemy

Battle of Moncontour 1569

was seen advancing, so that there was only time to take up position in a small hollow to shelter from the cannonade which lasted from eight in the morning until three in the afternoon. The Huguenots got the worst of it, and the Catholics then advanced, but their first line was beaten back. Then the powerful squadrons of German Black Troopers fighting for the Catholics – mercenaries were to be found on both sides – charged down on the Huguenots like a hurricane, and in less than half an hour the battle was over and the Huguenots *routed*. Among those who escaped in a skilfully led retreat was Walter Raleigh, then a young man of eighteen, fighting for the Huguenots with a 'gallant company' of English volunteers, 'nobly mounted and equipped'. In the picture you can see soldiers fighting round their 'colours' or flags which would be defended to the last. The victorious Catholics took two hundred colours at Moncontour.

Coligny had had his jaw broken by a pistol shot at the start of the battle. Now he was declared a traitor with a price of 50,000 *livres* on his head. He was hanged in *effigy* in Paris, his house was burnt down, his estates pillaged and his possessions sold by auction. Worse still, his army was broken and disbanded, over half having been killed at Moncontour, where the victorious army gave little *quarter* to the hated Huguenots. Yet Coligny never lost heart. 'Men have taken from us all they can,' he wrote, 'and as such is the good pleasure of God we will be content and happy.' He immediately set to work to restore the hopes and fortunes of his side, raising recruits in a remarkable march through the country. Before a year had passed, he had defeated a Catholic army more than twice the size of his own, and in the same year, 1570, forced the other side to make peace.

To try to make the peace of 1570 permanent, a marriage was planned between the Catholic princess Margaret, the king's sister, and the Huguenot prince, Henry of Navarre.

The family tree will show you a number of people who come into the story now.

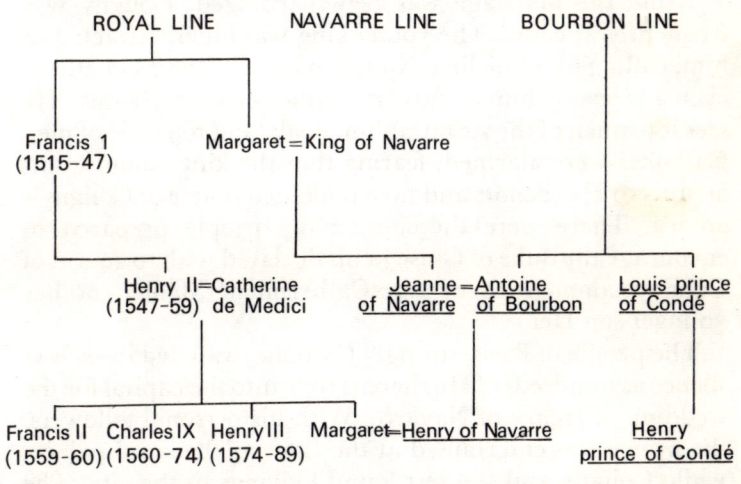

(Huguenots are underlined)

Born in the mountainous province of Béarn in the far south-west of France, prince Henry of Navarre had been brought up by his *eccentric* grandfather, and for some time lived in a castle near a small village, where he was 'clothed and fed like other children in that country. They even accustomed him to 25 run up and down the rocks. It is said that his ordinary food was brown bread, beef, cheese and garlic; and that they often made him walk barefoot and bareheaded.' Eighteen years old in 1572, the year of his marriage, Henry was tough and practical, yet lively and cheerful, with pleasant, easy manners. He had been present at Moncontour and at other battles, and already showed signs of military skill and courage.

People thought his bride, Margaret, really beautiful, with black hair, dark eyes and clear skin. She was, however, vain and spoilt like all the royal children. Her brother, Charles the king, was *unstable* and, at twenty-two, still under the influence of his mother, Catherine, a member of the famous, rich and clever Medici family of Florence in Italy. She was powerful at court, a great schemer and ambitious for her sons, especially her favourite, another Henry, later to succeed his brother as king Henry III of France. He was a Catholic and is not to be confused with Henry of Navarre.

While the marriage was being arranged, Coligny was frequently at court. The young king was much attracted to him, calling him 'the first captain of the age', and sometimes even addressing him as 'father'. Catherine grew jealous. 'He sees too much of the Admiral,' she said, 'and too little of me.' Catholics were alarmed, fearing that the king would grant favours to Huguenots and take too much notice of Coligny's advice. There were therefore many people prepared to encourage the duke of Guise in his declared wish to get rid of Coligny; amongst them were Catherine de Medici and her younger son Henry.

The people of Paris, strongly Catholic, watched in *ominous* silence as hundreds of Huguenots rode into the capital for the wedding of Henry of Navarre. With his personal followers, the prince was entertained at the Louvre, the royal palace, while Coligny and the rest found lodgings in the city. The ceremony took place on 18 August 1572, the bride wearing a dress of cloth of gold and rare lace, a blue *mantle* with a train four yards long, a cape of ermine and a *diadem* of precious stones. Even her handkerchief and gloves were trimmed with gold. Three days passed in feasting, balls and banquets. On the morning of the fourth day all seemed quiet. Coligny spent a few minutes watching his Huguenot son-in-law playing tennis with the king and the duke of Guise. Surely such a sight must mean the troubles between Catholics and Protestants were at an end. So Coligny may have thought as he left to return to his lodging only a few streets away from the palace. Someone handed him a letter, and as he slowly turned a corner reading it, two shots rang out. The Admiral staggered back. 'I am wounded,' he gasped.

Coligny's followers at once sounded the alarm. While some tended the wounded man, others rushed into the house from which the shots had been fired. They found an arquebus beside an open window, but the man had escaped. They learnt that he was one of Guise's followers. Henry of Navarre at once went to see Coligny, swearing to be revenged on those who had done the deed. The king too visited the Admiral who had just undergone a painful operation for the removal

Charles IX

27

of a bullet from his arm. Charles swore to find those responsible and have them punished. Catherine, the queen mother, who had accompanied her son, picked up the bullet removed by the surgeon, and slowly turned it round in her hand. The failure of the attempt to murder Coligny troubled her, for she feared the anger of the Huguenots when they found out by whose order that bullet had been fired. She looked around; there was the king already under the Admiral's influence again, listening to something whispered by the wounded man. Catherine hurried her son away.

The next day, Saturday, Paris was full of rumours and alarms. Huguenots, longing for action, were not sure what to do; no one knew for certain who was to blame for the attack on Coligny. The duke of Guise rode out of the city with great public show, returning in secret shortly afterwards. Many Huguenots thought it would be best to leave Paris, but Coligny was too weak to be moved, and not wanting to desert their leader, they did nothing but gather in groups to discuss the situation, which made Catholic citizens suspicious. Meanwhile, in the Louvre, Catherine had called her most trusted advisers together to discuss the crisis. All agreed that they would do right to use violence against the Huguenots who were said to be plotting against the king. Catherine undertook to get the consent of the king who finally broke down and gave in to her wishes. The duke of Guise and others planned the attack and when night fell loyal Catholics throughout Paris were ready – and waiting.

Catherine de Medici

4 St Bartholomew's Day

It was 24 August 1572, St Bartholomew's Day. Not long after midnight, Coligny was suddenly awakened by the clattering of horses' hooves on the cobbles outside. Someone knocked loudly on the door, crying 'Open in the king's name'. Hearing the noise of fighting below, Coligny asked his friends to

Massacre of St. Bartholomew, Paris, August 24 1572. The principal subject is the murder of Coligny. To the left the admiral is leaving the Louvre, and while reading a memorandum is wounded by an arquebus fired from a window (August 22); in the background, one of his equerries is communicating this fact to King Charles IX, whom he finds playing at tennis. To the right Coligny, attacked by soldiers in his hotel, is assassinated, and his body thrown from the window falls at the Duc de Guise's feet. In the next house other Protestants are being massacred.

The massacre of St. Bartholomew's Day by François Dubois

lift him out of bed, which was done. He said to them, 'I have long been prepared to die; but you must all flee for your lives if it be not too late. You cannot save me. I commit myself to God's mercy.' Soon the assassins burst in. 'Are you not the Admiral?' asked one, pointing his sword at Coligny's breast. 'I am,' replied Coligny calmly, 'but, young man, you should respect my grey hairs and not attack a wounded man.' The man, with an oath, plunged his sword into the Admiral's

breast and others savagely joined in the attack until Coligny
fell to the floor. They dragged his body to the window and
flung it down to the courtyard where Guise was waiting.
Someone wiped away the blood from the dead man's face.
'Yes, it is he; I know him well,' said Guise kicking the body
away. 'We have made a good beginning!'

A church bell rang out over the dark city, to be answered
almost at once by many more. From shadowy gateways and

courtyards armed men poured into the streets, breaking into known Huguenot houses and lodgings, rousing their defenceless victims from sleep and cutting or shooting them down as they fled. They murdered young and old, throwing bodies from windows, stabbing those who had fallen to the ground, tying up people still alive and dragging them through the streets to throw them in the river. Each murderer wore a white band round his arm and a white cross in his hat, and Catholics had placed lighted candles in their windows so that the terrible work might proceed more easily. When dawn came to dim the candles and give colour to the streams of blood in the streets, noblemen, high ranking officers, and priests with a crucifix in one hand and a sword in the other could be seen urging on the slaughter.

One bewildered twelve-year-old Huguenot boy was roused from sleep 'by the sound of all the bells and the confused cries . . .' He set out alone to seek shelter at the college where he had studied. He later described his nightmare journey through the city. 'I was seized with horror inexpressible at the sight of the furious murderers who, running from all points, forced open the houses and cried aloud, "Kill, kill, massacre the Huguenots". The blood which I saw shed before my eyes redoubled my terror.'

Three times the boy fell into the hands of bands of murderers, but each time was saved by the book of Catholic prayers which he had had the forethought to pick up before leaving his lodgings and which served him as a kind of passport. Finally he reached the college and was taken to the principal, but 'two inhuman priests . . . wanted to force me from him, that they might cut me to pieces, saying the order was not to spare even infants at the breast'. Fortunately the priests did not get their way and the boy was saved, to become in later years duke of Sully and chief minister of France. He remained a staunch Huguenot all his life.

There were terrible scenes too in the royal palace. Henry of Navarre and his cousin, the young prince of Condé, were roused just before dawn and told that the king wished to see them at once. With his mother and brother standing in the background, Charles advanced on them, crying, 'Mass or death!' Thus ordered to turn Catholic or die, Condé at once declared that he would not change his religion. Henry, with more caution, asked for time to consider. Both were forced to become Catholics and were kept at court almost as prisoners for the next four years.

At least the princes' lives were saved. Their servants and men-at-arms, however, were rounded up and their names checked against a list. As each man answered his name he was forced to enter a courtyard and make his way through a gruesome guard of honour of armed men who made short work of him with spear, sword and halberd. The princess Margaret, whose wedding a week before these men had come to attend, was awakened by a loud knocking. When her woman opened the door, thinking it was Henry of Navarre, a terrified gentleman in waiting pursued by four soldiers and bleeding from a sword cut, rushed in and threw himself on the princess's bed, clasping her in his arms to save his life. She jumped out of bed on the other side and he followed, still clinging to her. 'We both shouted out, being equally frightened,' she wrote afterwards. The Captain of the Guard who had just entered shouted too, with laughter, but he turned the soldiers out and the man, luckier than his companions, was saved.

The terror continued in Paris for most of the next week. There were some miraculous escapes, although these unfortunately were few. Those who did survive often owed their lives to quick thinking. A boy of thirteen, Jacques Caumont de la Force, was driven from a house with his father and brother who were both stabbed to death. Jacques, who by some miracle escaped the stabbing, had the presence of mind to cry out and fall down with them. Later some men came and robbed the bodies of their clothes, but Jacques made no movement. He was left with one stocking when a poor man came and took it off. 'Alas!' he said, 'what a pity! This is but a child, what can he have done?' Hearing a kind voice, Jacques raised his head and spoke to the man who told him to lie there till nightfall when he came to fetch him, putting a shabby cloak round him and passing him off as his own nephew. Thus the boy escaped; when he grew up he became a soldier and in the end a marshal of France.

The most hair-raising escape of all was that of Philippe du Plessis Mornay, a Huguenot nobleman who had been in Coligny's service. He had slept through the *tocsin* and on being roused by his terrified landlord, dressed himself, put on his sword and burnt his papers before jumping out of his bedroom window onto a roof below. Here he found a hiding-place behind a chimney until the danger passed. Next day assassins entered the street again, killed the Huguenot book-seller next door and threw his body down into the road with all his books and furniture. Philippe decided he must leave and, changing into plain black clothes, walked boldly out of the inn. He joined up with bands of murderers to avoid suspicion and was sad and angry on hearing them boast of the numbers they had killed. In this way he came to the house of his family lawyer, and calmly sat down in the office pretending to work with the clerks, while armed men were searching the premises. He was then concealed in a small room, but suspicion fell on the lawyer who was questioned.

Next day Philippe decided to leave and one of the lawyer's clerks bravely offered to take him through the nearest city gate where he had friends among the guards. They left in such a hurry that the clerk forgot to change his slippers. They could not get through the gate which was guarded, but talked their way through the next and set off with light hearts on the road to Normandy. They had only gone twenty paces when the guards of the gate noticed the clerk's slippers. However, they were allowed to go on but were stopped again at a village a little farther on. A crowd of workmen and others, declaring they were Huguenots, dragged them to the river to drown them. Here again they managed to talk their way out of danger and their accusers agreed to get a certificate from the clerk's employer who was, of course, Philippe's lawyer. This would confirm that Philippe was a clerk going to Rouen where his family lived. But at that moment a carriage arrived from Rouen and no one in it could recognise Philippe, so the two were again dragged to the river. 'If you really are a clerk, you will be able to read Latin,' shouted someone, bringing a book. Philippe who was well educated, at once began to read.

*Philippe
du Plessis Mornay*

'Why, you are a Huguenot doctor who will infect all Normandy!' they mocked him. 'To the water!' Luckily, at that moment the messenger arrived back with a note from the lawyer to say that Philippe was indeed his clerk, and was not a rebel nor against the government. (You will notice that the lawyer did not say he was not a Huguenot.) The note was enough to free the two young men and, after taking leave of the Catholic friend who had risked his life for him, Philippe escaped to Normandy and was soon on board a ship for England – a much safer place for him.

In France the massacre spread to the provinces where scenes similar to those in Paris took place. No one knows exactly how many Huguenots were slain at this time; one estimate is 20,000. Whatever the true figure, the number was terrible, for the victims were not killed in battle but murdered in cold blood, often with heartless tortures too. Civil war soon broke out again and although Coligny's leadership was badly missed, the Huguenots bravely resisted the Catholics' attempts to capture all their cities and towns and to grind

35

their faith away by terror and persecution. La Rochelle withstood a five-month siege and the little town of Sancerre in the central province of Berry held out from January till August 1573. The people were forced to eat leather, roots and even parchment. They could still read the writing on it when it was cooked and served at table! Gradually the Huguenots grew stronger and when Henry of Navarre escaped from court in 1576, he became a Huguenot again and was made their leader.

Henry III, the new king who had succeeded his brother in 1574, at first supported the Catholics, but soon became jealous of the duke of Guise who was called 'the king of Paris' because of his popularity there. Guise became so powerful that the king fled from the city, but soon he had his revenge. One day he sent for the duke who, all unsuspecting, walked along a dark passage to reach the king's room. Twenty men, stationed in the shadows, fell upon the duke and quickly killed him. 'Now I alone am king!' boasted Henry III. His mother Catherine was on her death-bed. She died two weeks after Guise, fearful of what would happen to her favourite son who had had the 'king of Paris' murdered. As she had feared Paris rose against the king, and a few months later he too died at the hand of an assassin. The year was 1589 and now, seventeen years after Coligny's murder and the terrible massacre which followed it, all those responsible were dead.

Assassination of Henry duke of Guise

5 Peaceful Arts

The Bastille

In the year before his death, Henry III the last of Catherine de Medici's sons to rule France, paid a visit to the Bastille, the grim fortress used to imprison enemies of the state. Among the prisoners were two young sisters and a frail old man; their only crime was their steadfast refusal to give up the Huguenot religion. The king urged the old man to become a Catholic, but he replied, 'These girls and I . . . have a part in the kingdom of heaven . . . all your people and yourself cannot compel a Potter to bow down to images of clay!' The girls were burnt at the stake, their courage an inspiration to the Huguenot soldiers still fighting in the terrible wars of religion. The old man, who died in the Bastille the following year, was Bernard Palissy, a potter whose art, skill and strength of character won him a fame that has endured.

Bernard Palissy lived at Saintes, the little town where Philibert Hamelin had founded a Huguenot church. After Hamelin's death, Palissy was one of the six members who kept the faith alive there. He had had hardly any education. 'I have had no other books than Heaven and Earth which are

37

open to all,' he said, but somehow he learnt to read and write and became a worker in stained glass, sometimes making a little extra money by painting portraits. Then one day he saw 'an earthen cup, turned and enamelled with so much beauty . . .' that he determined to discover the secret, as yet unknown in France, of the lovely *glaze*. 'Regardless of the fact that I had no knowledge of clays, I began to seek for the enamels as a man gropes in the dark,' he wrote. The task proved far more difficult than he had expected. At last he discovered how to make the white enamel, but could not get his kiln hot enough to melt it. He kept the kiln going for six days and nights, but nothing happened.

> I was getting desperate [he wrote]. Although I was *all in*, I realised that in my enamel I had not enough of the *ingredient* that helps the others to melt. Seeing this, I immediately began to smash and grind up this ingredient, at the same time seeing that my kiln did not get cold. When I had mixed my enamel I had to go and buy some more pots to try it out as I had lost all those I had made. When I had covered the new pots with enamel I put them in the kiln, still keeping the fire going. But then came more trouble for, the wood having run out, I was forced to burn the posts holding up the trellis in my garden. When this was burnt up I had to have the tables and floor-boards of the house to get the second mixture to melt. I was in such a state I did not know what to say for I was completely worn out and dried up by all the effort and the heat of the kiln. . . . The only comfort I got was to be jeered at and the very people who should have helped me went shouting round the town that I was burning up the floor, so that I lost all respect and was looked on as mad.

Palissy went through eight years of poverty and failure followed by another eight years of painful experiment before he perfected his art. His wife was naturally worried and showed him no sympathy. This is what he wrote about his most difficult times:

> For several years with nothing to cover my kilns I found myself every night at the mercy of the rain and wind with-

Bernard Palissy

out any help or consolation except for the hooting of the owls on the one side and dogs howling on the other. Sometimes the wind got up and the storm was so great, blowing on my kilns above and below that I was forced to leave everything and so lose the fruit of my labour. And sometimes when I had had to leave it all without a dry stitch on me I would go off to bed at midnight or break of day looking like a man who had been dragged through all the mud of the town, staggering along with no candle and filled with the blackest thoughts. Then in my bedroom I would find waiting for me a persecution worse than the first, so great that it is now a marvel to me that I was not completely overcome. [He meant that his wife scolded him bitterly.]

At last a great nobleman employed him to make enamelled tiles to decorate his new castle. Hardly had Palissy begun the work than his workshop was wrecked in anti-Huguenot riots and he was imprisoned. The nobleman, impatient to have his castle finished, secured royal protection for Palissy and so he was appointed 'Inventor of *Rustic Figulines*' to the king.

In his work Palissy often made use of designs from nature, as in the beautiful dish in the illustration. This shows a river with eels swimming in it, a lizard on dry ground and, on the rim of the dish, leaves and plants growing on the bank. Everything was modelled in clay and then enamelled in the bright colours which Palissy had discovered after so much hard work. The subjects are most realistic for he was a great naturalist, having taught himself by careful observation.

Pottery dish by Palissy

When he had finished the nobleman's castle, Palissy went to Paris to work for Catherine the queen mother, to decorate her new palace, the Tuileries. Here he made enamelled pottery statuettes, vases, cups, plates, and tiles to line the artificial caves or grottoes which were very popular in gardens in those days. A document in the National Library in Paris shows a payment made in 1570 'to Bernard, Nicolas and Mathurin Palissy sculptors in earth, the sum of 2,600 livres for all the works in earth, baked and enamelled, which remain to be done for the completion of the . . . grotto commenced for the queen in her palace'. Nicolas and Mathurin were two of Palissy's sons who were now working with their father. He himself was still working for Catherine when the

40

massacre of St Bartholomew's day took place. His life was spared, probably because she knew no one else could complete the work he had begun.

In Paris Palissy made many friends among scholars and scientists who came to hear him give lectures about his work as a naturalist and on other topics which interested him, such as waters and fountains, metals, salts, stones, earths, fire and enamels. No one, however, could save him from later persecution, and thus it was that one of the great artists of his day – an artist in earth as he called himself – died in the Bastille.

Bernard Palissy died in 1589. It was the same year, as we have seen, as the deaths of Catherine the queen mother and her son Henry III who left no children. By the French law of succession, the crown now passed to the late king's cousin, Henry of Navarre, heir in his own right. He had also married Margaret, Catherine's daughter, although the marriage had long since gone 'on the rocks'. But would France accept a Huguenot king? Henry of Navarre, or Henry IV as his followers now called him, soon found that it would not, and that he must go on fighting. 'I am a king without a kingdom, a husband without a wife, and a warrior without money,' he lamented.

Henry's dismal mood did not last long for he soon defeated his Catholic enemies, now in alliance with Spain, at the battles of Arques (1589) and Ivry (1590). One of his most devoted followers was the man best known by his later title, the duke of Sully who, after recovering from wounds received at Ivry, joined the king outside Paris. Henry had laid siege to the capital but could not bear to see the sufferings of his starving people. As his enemies were also pressing, he withdrew, but three years later the strongly Catholic city was still refusing to accept him as king. Sully, *devout* Huguenot though he was, felt that there was only one thing to be done. 'I resolved,' he wrote, 'to *prevail upon* the king to embrace the Roman Catholic faith.' It took three days to persuade the king, but the thought of winning the capital finally convinced him. 'Paris is worth a Mass,' he is reported to have said. Many Huguenots felt betrayed, some even left the king's service, but Sully managed to show the rest how

41

Henry IV entering Paris

essential Henry's conversion was. In July 1593, Henry, dressed in white satin with a black mantle, made his way to the church of Saint Denis just outside Paris where a Catholic archbishop received him with the words, 'Who are you?' 'I am the king,' replied Henry. 'What is your demand?' 'I require to be received . . . into the Roman Church.' 'Do you wish it sincerely?' 'Yes,' said the king, 'I wish and I desire it. I protest and swear in the face of the Almighty to live and die in the Catholic religion.'

It was not until 1598 that Henry became the undisputed master of his kingdom; but at last all his enemies made terms. Now it was time to remember his old friends and although some Catholics objected, Henry gave a charter of liberties to the Huguenots. The Edict of Nantes, as it was called, gave them the right to worship in the Protestant fashion wherever they had done so before, although not in Paris or in certain other strongly Catholic towns. They could have their own law courts even in Catholic districts as well as schools in their own districts, while their children also had the right to attend Catholic schools. All jobs were to be open to Huguenots, and they were even to have some seats reserved for them in the

Royal Council. Money was to be given each year to pay Huguenot ministers who could meet together to discuss religious affairs at gatherings called Synods, every three years. Finally, the Huguenots were allowed to have their own towns. There were 150 of these, many of which could be fortified, and garrisoned with Protestant soldiers paid by the king but under the control of a Protestant governor. The map shows that the greatest number of Huguenot towns was in the south and west of France. The most important ones are named.

Protestant towns in 1600

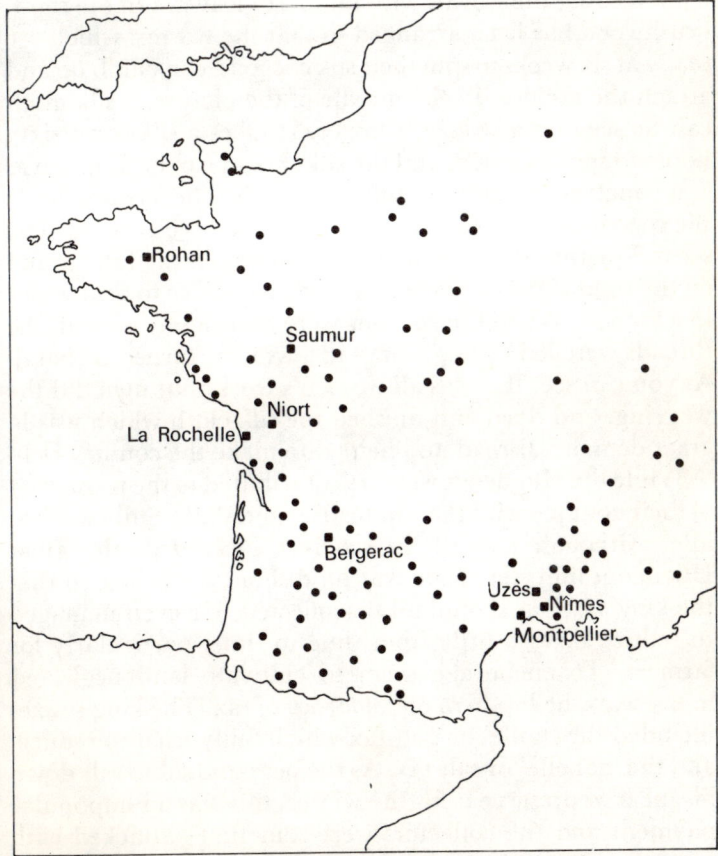

In the task of restoring their ruined country after the long wars, Huguenots played an important part, for they were hardworking and often skilled craftsmen and farmers. Many Huguenots were weavers of woollen cloth or other materials such as linen. Carpets and tapestries were also made, with intricate designs. Henry IV was particularly keen to encourage the silk industry, and had silk-worms imported, and leaflets distributed in the south of France where mulberry trees could be grown. (Do you know why silk-worms and mulberry trees go together?)

The first of these two pictures, engraved in Henry's reign, shows a 'magnanerie' or 'silkwormery'. The woman on the left is feeding the worms with mulberry leaves. On the right, brushwood has been arranged so that the worms, which are ready at six weeks to spin their silk cocoons, can climb up and attach themselves. In the middle of the picture, a silk moth can be seen on a woman's finger. It takes a silkworm sixty hours to spin its *cocoon*, and the silk thread can be as much as 1,500 metres – not quite a mile – in length. The *chrysalis* inside the cocoon is killed by heat, and the thread is unwound. The second picture shows how this was done. In the foreground on the right a girl can be seen stoking a furnace to heat water in a trough. When the cocoons were thoroughly soaked, the threads were led through rings to a winder, turned by hand. As you can see, this was all women's work; but men did the weaving, and dyed and finished the silk cloth which was in great demand abroad and helped to make the country rich.

While the Huguenot workers contributed to the prosperity of their country with their industries and skills, Sully was not idle. Although not all his schemes succeeded, the great Huguenot minister made war on dishonest officials, so that the king's *revenue* should all be collected. He even managed to reduce taxes a little from time to time, particularly for farmers. To encourage them to cultivate land neglected in the wars, he let them off all *arrears* of tax. The king's taxes included the 'taille' or poll-tax which Sully tried to reduce, and the 'gabelle' or salt tax. As the peasant had to salt down his meat to preserve it for the winter, this was an unpopular payment and the collectors were sometimes attacked with

A magnanerie

Unwinding the cocoons

Sully

pitchforks or guns. The peasant also had to pay *tithes* to the Church, which meant one sheaf of corn in every ten, and often a tenth of other produce. Huguenots had to pay tithes too, even though they were against the Catholic Church. When royal taxes and church tithes had been paid, the peasants still had many dues to pay to their lords, for instance for the use of a cornmill, a winepress and even a bread oven.

Many lords despised their peasants and did nothing to help them, but Henry IV realised how hard life could be for them and made a law forbidding nobles to ride across peasants' cornfields. By the end of his reign, because of the king's efforts, some improvements had been made in the condition of the poor. Sometimes when Henry was out hunting he would leave his followers and knock on the door of a peasant's cottage; then, invited to take a drink inside, the plainly dressed visitor would ask how the crops and cattle were doing, and as the conversation went on, would ask his host what he thought of the king. Henry seems to have been seldom recognised, but he usually heard himself praised, for

Henry of Navarre

the peasants knew that the king really cared about his subjects and wanted them to be happy. Everywhere he became known as 'le bon Henri' – Henry the good.

Many Huguenots who had fought for Henry in the wars of religion now farmed their own smallholdings; their fears were no longer of persecution and battle, but of drought, floods or failure of crops. Symbolically some had turned their armour into cooking pots! One of these retired soldiers was Agrippa d'Aubigné who had left Henry's service in disgust when the king turned Catholic, but never quite lost his affection for him. Agrippa, who was born in Saintonge near La Rochelle, retired to the nearby province of Poitou to rebuild his house and cultivate his land. Here in the west, away from the busy capital and court, he could live simply and quietly, as he desired. He was also one of the greatest French poets of his time, and this sonnet on the good life (here translated from the French original), must express the feelings of many Huguenots like himself during the generally peaceful and prosperous years of Henry IV and Sully.

Agrippa d'Aubigné

D'you want to know what things give life its worth
My merry d'Aubigné? Such things are these:
Not what we get by toil but find with ease,
Good healthy food, warm fire and fruitful earth,

No case at law, no strife; a soul of mirth,
A body fit, not thin nor yet *obese*;
No crafty tricks, yet no stupidities,
Congenial friends, of dainty dish no *dearth*,

No cause for fear or doubt, a purse well lined,
A sprightly wife of the fair and faithful kind;
A sleep unspoilt by snores, a rest sincere

To shorten night and leave tired eyes behind,
True to yourself, just taking what you find,
Attached to life, flee death, but not in fear.

6 Siege and Surrender

May 14, 1610, was a warm day. Henry IV, king of France, was restless and at about four in the afternoon decided to visit Sully who was unwell. As the coach, open on both sides, left the Louvre, a man quickly began to follow it on foot. A little further on, two carts, one loaded with barrels of wine and the other piled with hay, blocked the narrow street. As the king's men ran forward to remove the obstructions, the man who had been following came alongside and, placing one foot on the front wheel and the other on a stone at the side of the road, aimed a violent blow at the king with a knife.

Ravaillac murders Henry IV, and (background r. to l.) is tortured and executed.

Henry cried out, but those with him in the coach seemed paralysed with surprise or fear. A second blow pierced the royal victim to the heart and although a third attack was turned aside by an attendant it was too late to save the king. The assassin, Francois Ravaillac, still had the knife in his hand when seized. Later, he declared he had killed Henry because the king had planned to fight on the Protestant side in a war in Germany. Tortured and condemned to a horrible death, Ravaillac justified his act as that of a good Catholic. Most Frenchmen, however, Catholics and Protestants alike, deeply mourned the death of 'le bon Henri', who had done so much for his country. Their feelings were expressed by the Huguenot poet d'Aubigné who declared himself heart-broken when he heard the news.

D'Aubigné had other reasons also to regret the death of Henry IV, for his successors were not so sympathetic towards the Huguenots. Within a few months the great minister Sully had been dismissed and had retired to his estates, and after ten troubled years d'Aubigné himself became involved in a revolt and was exiled from France. The Protestant city of

Richelieu

Geneva received him with honour and he was able to buy a house and marry again after twenty-five years as a widower. For another ten years he led the kind of happy life he had described in his sonnet; then, in 1630, he met 'death without fear' and with a psalm on his lips as so many of his fellow Huguenot warriors had done, although, unlike most of them, he died in his bed.

Back in France the years 1620 to 1630 had been unhappy for the Huguenots. Many had died in battle or as a result of long sieges in the renewed struggle between Protestants and Catholics. The Huguenots were defiant and warlike as they faced the Catholic government of the new king, Louis XIII, and sought alliances with the enemies of France. This made the king's intelligent and determined minister, *Cardinal* Richelieu, decide to take away their political and military power. He proved a cool and resolute enemy to the Protestant cause. There was fighting in many parts of France, but the battle to the death took place in La Rochelle.

The picture shows seventeenth-century French merchants *transacting* business in a busy port where many ships are

Merchants

unloading cargoes or sailing in and out of harbour. Such was the daily scene in La Rochelle, a city which owed its wealth and importance to sea-borne trade. It is quite easy for a presentday visitor to La Rochelle to picture the city as it was in the days of the rich Huguenot merchants, for as the incoming tide covers the mud flats of the long channel, it brings the smell of seaweed and salt water right into the heart of the old city, as it did when the magnificent houses and the harbour walls were first built. There is a fine town hall and inside is a marble table chipped at one edge.

Merchants' houses in La Rochelle

In those days the harbour would be *thronged* with ships. Vessels from West Africa, with gold dust and rubber, and the West Indian fleet, bringing sugar, coffee, vanilla and cocoa, would be docked alongside Dutch or English ships, with their more commonplace cargoes of salted meat and fish, bales of linen and woollen cloth. Locally owned vessels back from North Africa with dates and almonds would come in on the same tide as the ships from Lisbon carrying spices, precious stones and perfumes imported from the East by the Portuguese. Then, laden with the famous wines of France or with salt, a local product of great value, the ships would soon be out on the tide to bring yet more wealth to their enterprising owners. Business was not without risk, for ships were very small by our standards and at the mercy of wind and wave. Delays would be expensive and losses tragic and sometimes ruinous; yet when the account books were balanced, the businesslike Huguenot merchants nearly always came out on the *credit side*. Unfortunately, their successes made the Catholics jealous and even more inclined to hate the Huguenots.

In 1620 Jean Guiton became one of the city's magistrates. He was one of the chief shipowners and had often been on trading voyages himself so that, when La Rochelle rose in revolt against the king, he was made admiral of the Huguenot rebel fleet. Guiton was constantly in action against the king's ships and several times attacked fleets much larger than his own, sometimes with success, and always with courage and determination. In 1625 he fought his way desperately out of La Rochelle rather than surrender to a large royal fleet. In spite of heavy losses he reached the English coast with twenty-two ships.

Protestant England was an obvious refuge for the hard-pressed Huguenots from La Rochelle, even though the king, Charles I, had just married Henrietta Maria, sister of the king of France. Early in his reign, Charles agreed to send some ships to help his brother-in-law against the Huguenot rebels, but the English sailors mutinied and refused to fight against their fellow Protestants. Charles I then quarrelled with Louis XIII, and by 1627 England was at war with France and eager to help the Huguenots in their rebellion.

53

Under the command of Charles's favourite, the Duke of Buckingham, an English fleet set out for La Rochelle. Buckingham, although brave, was a poor organiser and his expedition was badly supplied and short of arms and ammunition. The soldiers he landed on the island of Ré just outside La Rochelle were rogues or untrained village *yokels* who could not subdue the strongly built fort there. Richelieu now arrived wearing, to the amusement of some onlookers, armour on top of his priestly robes and carrying a *rapier* beneath his cardinal's red cloak. By clever use of his ships and troops he routed the English force. As Buckingham sailed back to England with the remnants of his army, he turned to a French prisoner and said, 'Your Cardinal is the greatest man in the world!'

The great man now turned to the problem of defeating the rebels in La Rochelle who, encouraged by the arrival of the English, had closed the city gates against the king's troops. The citizens were confident that they would always be able to get supplies by sea, for they counted on help from England as well as on their own fleet commanded by Jean Guiton. Safe from attack by the king's ships, trading vessels would still be able to sail up the narrow channel into the city. Richelieu was determined to cut off La Rochelle from the sea and force surrender; he decided to build a huge dyke right across the channel. The task was tremendous but Richelieu inspired his men to work day and night. First, two hundred *hulks* were sunk in a line across the harbour, making a bridge of boats. Then the dyke was built up from each side. Such was the enthusiasm, that at one time the king of France himself was carrying stones alongside his men in a winter gale. The citizens watched with dismay as the gap in the middle became steadily smaller to be finally closed with ships sunk in the form of a triangle with its *apex* towards the sea. Cannon were mounted at many points and by the spring of 1628 the work was complete.

The situation inside the city had now become very grim. After nine months of siege the council, seeking a resolute leader, called on Jean Guiton to be mayor. He said, 'I will be your mayor since you press me, but only on condition that I

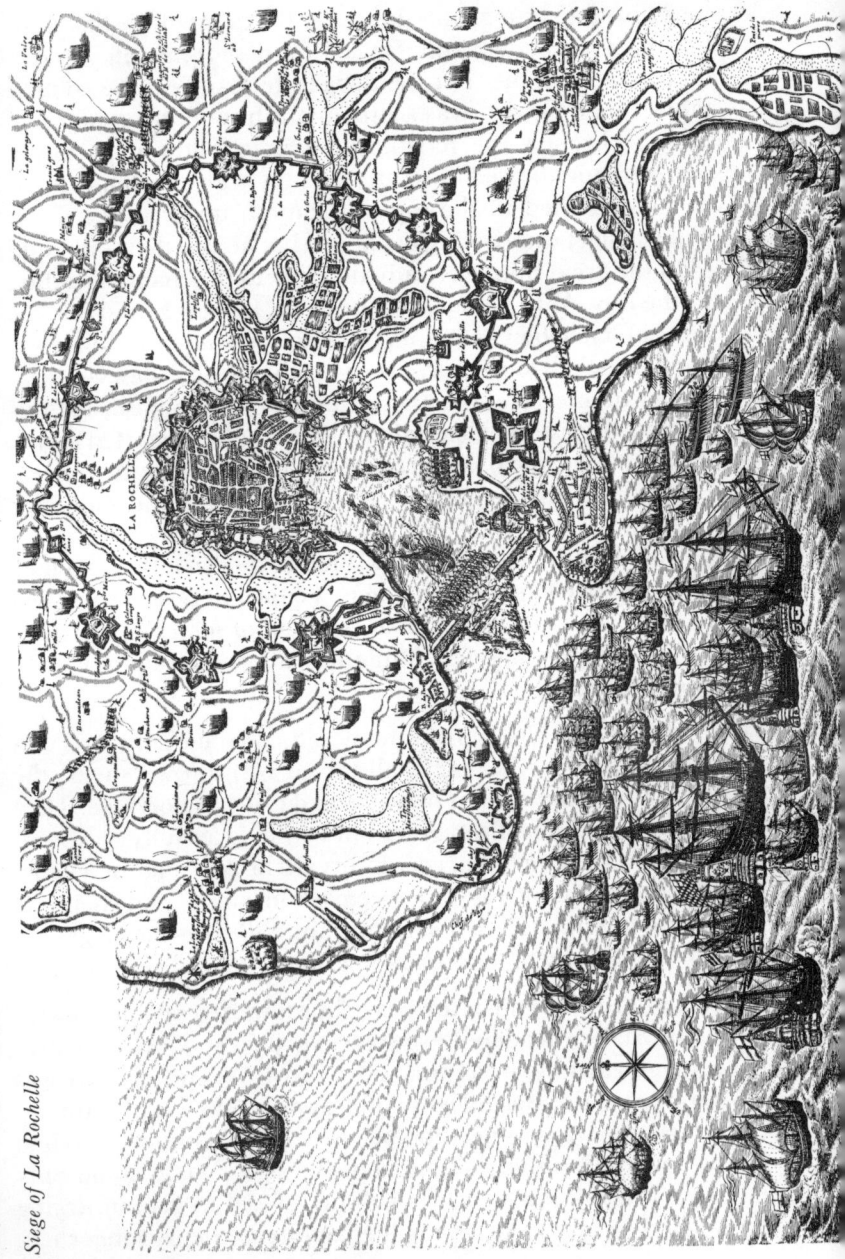

Siege of La Rochelle

be allowed to plunge this dagger in the heart of the first man to talk of surrender; and if ever I propose it myself, you can do the same to me. Let the dagger lie ready on the council table!' Jean Guiton was a little man, but of unconquerable spirit. Through the terrible days that followed he never wavered nor allowed those around him to give up hope. Each day he climbed to the top of a church tower to see if the English fleet was coming back. In May he saw their sails, and soon the great ships were advancing into the channel leading to the city. When they saw the dyke, however, and felt the force of Richelieu's cannon, the English prudently withdrew out of range. 'Do not leave your brothers . . .' began Guiton's desperate message, but there was little the English, led this time by the Earl of Denbigh, could do. A half-hearted attack was made on the dyke, greeted with wild joy by the towns-people; but the English fleet again drew off and sailed for home.

Despair settled on the city. What had been a thriving port now seemed like a ghost town. People were forced to eat horses, dogs and cats. When this sort of food ran out they turned to anything which might contain the slightest scrap of nourishment:

> From odd bits of parchment, old marriage contracts and scraps of leather belts, all mixed with brown sugar, the women made a sort of sweetened gruel or porridge. They *concocted* jellies from glue. They would carefully scrape off the hair from bits of cow-hide with broken glass or a knife, soak them in water for twenty-four hours, and then boil them with tallow for a long time. Before the siege was over, the people were eating boots and hats.

Towards the end of the siege, four hundred people are said to have fallen dead in the streets every day, and those left alive had not even the strength to bury them. Whenever there was an alarm, the defenders would appear, slow and panting, dragging weapons now too heavy to carry. Guiton, who had lost two of his five daughters in the siege, could stand only with the aid of a stick, yet still he refused to give in, trying always to inspire in others the confidence he no longer felt, that help must again be on its way from England. In September 1628, more than a year after the siege had begun, he heard that Buckingham was dead—stabbed by a discontented English soldier in a Portsmouth tavern while trying to organise another expedition to La Rochelle.

Guiton refused to surrender. Picking up the dagger from the council table, he flung it down again in a gesture of defiance. The point chipped the marble surface . . .

At the end of another month the English appeared again and bombarded the dyke, but, failing to *breach* it, decided to sue for peace. Richelieu was victorious and La Rochelle lost. The great gates were opened and the drawbridge lowered for the first time for fourteen terrible months. Twelve members of the city council, like shadows of living men, emerged to make their submission. Guiton was not among them, but when the Cardinal entered the city the next day, he met him with six archers. Richelieu told him he was no longer mayor and the king advised him to 'seek a change of air for a little while'. Guiton went to England, though hardly with grateful feelings in his heart.

Now Richelieu showed his greatness, for while the city lost its privileges, fortifications and Huguenot council, few people were killed, and even Guiton and his fellow councillors were banished only for six months. Although the Cardinal celebrated mass in the once-proud Huguenot city, he allowed the Protestants to keep their churches, their pastors and their own services. People who had feared that the city would be burnt or put to the sword, crept out to find that instead wagonloads of food had arrived. The garrison was spared and marched or rather staggered pitifully out— seventy-four French and sixty-two English soldiers were all that remained alive. Of the city's 28,000 inhabitants only 5,400 survived the siege; of these 1,000 soon died from its effects. No one felt any love for the English whose fleet was still anchored outside the harbour. A few days later, peace was made and they sailed for home. That night, as if to mock the defeated Huguenots, heavy seas at last broke through Richelieu's dyke.

7 Persecution

If you leave La Rochelle by the road that leads to Paris you will come, after about a hundred miles, to the city of Poitiers where the great preacher Calvin is said to have first declared himself a Protestant in 1533. The province of Poitou, of which Poitiers is the capital, was strongly Protestant in the sixteenth and seventeenth centuries and was the home of thousands of ordinary Huguenot families like the Migaults about whose escape from France you read in the first chapter of this book.

Jean Migault was an educated man who served as lawyer and schoolmaster for his Huguenot community. The picture of a seventeenth-century school is by a Huguenot artist, Abraham Bosse, who died in 1676. Perhaps Migault's school was rather like this, although as he lived in a village, the room would probably have been much smaller. Here is a translation of the French words under the picture:

> Hardened to his pupils' din, this able schoolmaster teaches with the aid of a birch.
> Some, strangely, obey through fear and learn their lessons with a tearful face.
> But with the others it is quite different. In frolicsome mood, they think only of the games they are going to play. Now you, who make fun of their games, must know that these children are perfectly innocent, and just remember that when you were a child you liked to do the same!

Migault's own family provided his school with quite a few pupils! Here is a complete list of his children:

Anne born 19 February 1664
Louis born 20 March 1665, died 1 June same year

A seventeenth-century schoolroom

Jeanne born 12 March 1667
Jacques born 3 April 1668
Gabriel born 22 June 1669
Jean born 2 September 1670
Philémon born 14 October 1671
Madeleine born 3 November 1673, died aged 11 years
Louis born 4 January 1675
Pierre born 5 May 1676
Marie born 16 July 1678
Elisabeth born 9 February 1680
René born 5 August 1681, died aged 3 months
Olivier born 21 February 1683

You will notice that some of the children had died young. This, unfortunately, was quite common in the seventeenth century as so little was known about medicine in those days. The surviving Migault children seem to have been healthier than most; they were to need all their strength to face the terrible hardships in store for them.

While Richelieu lived there had been no active persecution of Protestants, although many Catholic preachers were sent into Huguenot districts to try to *convert* them. They included many Jesuits, so called because they belonged to the Society of Jesus which had been founded by the Spaniard, Ignatius Loyola, in the sixteenth century. The society was organised like an army, fighting to bring people back into the Catholic Church. Jesuits were great preachers and teachers and their influence spread through many countries. They used other methods too which made them hated and feared, for some of them would stop at nothing to achieve their aims. The preachers had a little success, but not even the Jesuits could shake the faith of firm Huguenots like Jean Migault. Later he and his fellow Protestants were offered money to become Catholics. In 1670 Paul Pellisson, a *convert* himself, set up *bureaux* offering anything from seven francs upwards to encourage others to follow his example. The money which represented a week or two's wages was provided by the Catholic Church, and in twelve years the bureaux claimed 58,130 conversions. Rich Protestants soon set up rival bureaux to convert people back again, and some clever rogues were 'converted' several times.

Soon Migault and his friends heard some disturbing news, for in one or two places temples were being pulled down and Huguenot colleges and hospitals closed. Although the Edict of Nantes guaranteed toleration and civil rights to the Protestants, Catholic lawyers were now busy twisting its meaning to leave as little freedom as possible. The Edict gave the Huguenots the right to worship wherever they had done so before. The lawyers claimed that this must mean the actual buildings, with the result that any churches built after the Edict were pulled down. The Edict gave Huguenots a general right to enter trades and professions, but obviously could not mention every occupation by name. In the 1670s all whose profession was not actually named in the Edict were deprived of their jobs, even tailors, shoemakers and midwives.

Most disturbing of all for Huguenot parents were the attempts to convert their children. If a father had to go away, from fear of persecution perhaps, he often found on his return that his wife and family had been taken into Catholic convents or orphanages. When this happened to one Huguenot, Alexandre de St Michel, he promptly rescued his family and fled with them to England, where his beautiful daughter Elisabeth became, at the age of fifteen, the wife of Samuel Pepys, the famous diarist. In 1681 the French government declared that children of seven were old enough to change their religion, and soon Huguenot children were being bribed or forced to say they would become Catholics, then taken away from their parents in case they should become Protestants again. This led many Huguenots to flee abroad for fear of losing their children.

Jean Migault, like his fellow Huguenots, feared for his children. He had other worries too in this year 1681, for he had to close his school and also lost his legal work which was now forbidden to Huguenots. He was invited to become *reader* and *scribe* at a church in a small neighbouring town. He accepted, to the great anger of the Catholic priest or curé of his new district, who threatened, 'in language the most furious' as Migault wrote, to involve him in utter ruin if he came to live there. The curé was to carry out his threat, for it was in this town of Mougon that the Migault family experienced the terrible persecution known as the 'dragonnade'.

The dragonnade got its name from the *dragoons* who in the autumn of 1681 were sent into Poitou and *billeted* in the houses of Protestants. 'With *Papists*', wrote Migault, 'they were never known to dwell.' Although they had no written orders, the soldiers knew very well that they were expected to make life so unbearable for the Huguenots that they would speedily accept conversion to get rid of their persecutors. The brutal scheme worked in a lot of cases, but some brave Protestants would not give in, in spite of terrible hardships. People were driven from their homes like a woman whom Migault met

> hurrying across the country with three children, one at the breast, the others holding her hand. Her consternation cannot be described; she knew not whither she was bending her steps, and, fancying herself pursued by troopers, she would not slacken her pace, nor give any other answer to enquiries than that she dared not stop. . . . This pious·lady passed many nights in the open country, without shelter and for the most part *destitute* of food.

A few days later a troop of cavalry entered Mougon and soon two soldiers arrived at Migault's house demanding a meal which, wrote Migault, 'without exaggeration was to consist of more dishes than would suffice for twenty people.' Soon more and still more soldiers came, directed to Migault's house by his enemy the curé, until there were fifteen altogether. While Migault was out seeking provisions, the soldiers forced his wife to serve them with food and wine, and then, presumably for sport, subjected her to the ordeal known as 'roasting'. Migault who heard the story later, described it thus:

> One of them [the soldiers] having violently kicked her, forced the poor creature back into the sitting-room. The man then suggested that it would be proper to guard her and keep her warm. She was thrust into a corner of the fireplace while an immense fire was lighted. The soldiers even used some of the furniture for firewood . . . threaten-

Dragoon

ing to burn their victim unless she immediately renounced Protestantism. So *intolerable* was the heat that the men felt themselves unable to remain near the fire, and the person who was placed close to her was relieved every two or three minutes. This admirable woman, knowing in whom she believed, did not for a moment lose the *composure* of her mind. She cast all her cares and sufferings upon her Saviour; *repelled* the repeated *importunities* to change her religion with equal mildness and resolution until, *swooning* away, she became insensible to further insult and injury.

Some friendly Catholic neighbours, horrified at what was happening, had thrown themselves at the soldiers' feet imploring them to spare their victim, but with no effect. At last, however, a Catholic priest (not the curé) managed to stop them, and the neighbours took her to their own home and hid her in a corn loft saying that she had escaped. The furious soldiers searched for her in vain and, failing to find

63

her, destroyed or sold everything the Migaults possessed. Soon the Protestants in Mougon had either been 'converted' or had fled to the woods nearby.

Having destroyed all they could, the soldiers moved on to the next town and the Huguenots crept back home. The Migault children who returned from the homes of friends and relations were unfortunately in the town when the dragoons returned two months later. On this occasion Madame Migault managed to hide in time, but the soldiers picked up five-year-old Pierre who was crying and 'threw him with violence from one end of the apartment to the other'. Luckily the child was not much hurt but was terribly frightened and was later found wandering dazed in the garden.

You will be wondering who gave orders that women should be kicked and 'roasted', and little children thrown across a room and scared out of their wits. French Protestants, surprisingly, did not blame the king, for they felt that if only he knew what was happening to his loyal subjects he would stop the persecution. Louis XIV, thought by some to be the greatest king France ever had, spent most of his time leading his armies to war or living in his great palace at Versailles a

Louis XIV

Versailles

little way out of Paris. The palace was packed with treasures and works of art, and courtiers almost worshipped the 'sun king' as he was called. Louis worked hard at governing the country and enjoyed hunting, feasting, the theatre, picnics and fancy dress balls. Later in life he became increasingly religious as he fell under the influence of a remarkable woman, Madame de Maintenon, whom he secretly married in 1684. He began to regret his earlier gay and immoral life and his succession of beautiful mistresses, and wanted to do some service to the Church to make amends. Jesuits and Catholic priests were quick to suggest a suitable task: the conversion of all the Huguenots!

Once Louis had agreed, the methods of conversion were left to others. The king had once spoken of 'a little gentle and effective violence' but his Jesuit *confessor* Père (father) Lachaise and the minister in charge of the army, the Marquis of Louvois, were prepared to authorise far more. We can still

Louvois

read some letters in which Louvois gave orders that no violence was to be used against the Huguenots, but in others, although Louvois was careful not to put much on paper, you can see how persecution was slyly encouraged. Here is part of a letter addressed to the governor of Poitou by Louvois in 1681.

His Majesty has ordered me to send a regiment of cavalry into Poitou at the beginning of November, which is to be billeted on the Protestants. But he does not consider it necessary to quarter all the troops on them; for example, if, by a fair distribution, the Protestants would have had ten of the twenty-six sections making up a company, you can see to it that they have twenty instead and that they are quartered on the richest Protestants, giving as your excuse that when there are not sufficient troops in one place for all to have some, it is only fair that the poor should be exempt and the rich *encumbered*. Further, His Majesty has been pleased to execute the *ordinance* I send in which he commands that all converts be exempted from billeting troops for a period of two years. This ordinance contains the power to produce many converts in the staging towns if you see to it that it is well executed and that in the distribution of the troops passing through, the greater number are always billeted on the richest Protestants. But as I explained above, it is His Majesty's desire that the orders to the mayors and aldermen of the various localities, given either by you or your subordinates, should be by word of mouth only, without letting it be thought that His Majesty seeks to do violence to the Huguenots by compelling their conversion.

Local officials, like Marillac, the governor who received the letter, were often the keenest of all to persecute the Protestants. They were often urged on to great brutality by Catholic priests like the curé of Mougon. A number of ordinary Catholics joined in, enriching themselves by buying up the property that Protestants were forced to sell at rock bottom prices when fleeing the country. Some goods were just seized and stolen. It is only fair to say, however, that a good many

Catholics, like Migault's neighbours, gave shelter to the unfortunate Huguenots and helped them as much as they could.

For a short time after the first dragonnade in Poitou it looked as if the persecution might be eased, for when Huguenot complaints at last got through to the government, Marillac was dismissed. Louvois who wanted the persecution carried out more quietly said that Marillac had ignored his instructions that the Huguenots should have no *legitimate* grounds for complaint. The new governor, Basville, proved to be even worse than Marillac so the king was soon delighted to hear of many more conversions in Poitou. He was probably not told what was really going on, but should have found out what was being done in his name, for to many people throughout the world the name of Louis XIV was becoming a symbol of tyranny and barbarity.

The Migaults were forced to leave Poitou, and soon afterwards, in 1683, Madame Migault died of a fever after giving birth to Olivier. Her dying thoughts were for her children whom she commended to her husband's 'greatest care'. Her last words were, 'Heaven be praised my love, I am strong in faith. I die happy.' Jean Migault's difficulties increased after this and he was forced to send his children to hiding-places as persecution was resumed. He became a *fugitive*. He wrote: 'I wandered up and down the province, concealing myself in the day and never staying more than forty-eight hours in the same house.' Thousands of Huguenots who still clung to their faith at that time – October 1685 – were living the same kind of hunted life.

8 Revocation, Slavery and Revolt

By October 1685 Louis XIV's advisers were telling him that it would only be a matter of time before there were no Protestants left in France. Catholic lawyers whose actions had gradually destroyed the Huguenots' rights and liberties were asking what was the use of keeping the document which had originally guaranteed them. Influenced by these arguments and longing to complete the conversion of the Huguenots, Louis in this month *revoked* the Edict of Nantes.

Although the Huguenots had been persecuted for many years, the Revocation came as a great blow because it destroyed their last hope of being able to worship as they wished. Many thought at once of leaving the country, but the government, fearing to lose more skilled workers, forbade this. Huguenots were expected to become Catholics and settle down and, so that they should have no religious leaders to encourage them to do otherwise, Protestant ministers were ordered to leave France within fifteen days. In the years that followed the Edict, ministers faced death for trying to stay in the country to help their flocks, while any other Huguenots caught trying to flee would be sentenced to the *galleys* for life. The first part of this chapter tells the story of one such Huguenot and describes the galleys and the men aboard them.

Jean Marteilhe was only ·sixteen when, in 1700, the dragoons came to his province of Périgord. He fled but was captured trying to cross the frontier into the Netherlands. When all attempts to convert him failed he was sent to the galleys at Dunkirk. In a book he wrote many years later, after he had gained his freedom, Marteilhe described the

French galley

galleys in great detail:

A Galley is ordinarily an hundred and Fifty feet long and forty broad; it has but one Deck and its Hold is divided into six Apartments. There are on the Deck sixty seats for the Rowers or Galley slaves and six Slaves to each Seat. The Oars are fifty Feet long, thirteen of which are within, the rest without the Vessel. The Deck is separated in the Middle by a Range of Timbers running from Stem to Stern called the Coursier, composed of thick Planks of Oak which form a sort of continued Chest or Case to hold the Tents and other Baggage of the Crew. This Case or Chest is covered by other Boards laid cross-ways and forms a sort of Walk, with Seats on the right and left. A Galley has two Masts, the Main mast which is fixed in the Centre of the Vessel is 60 Feet high and without *Shrouds* to ascend it. The Sailors are expert at climbing it with the Assistance only of a single Rope. The *Sailyard* is twice as long as the mast and consequently an hundred and twenty Feet long. The *Mizen*-mast which is fixed at the Prow is forty Feet high. Its Sail-yard is eighty Feet long.

Another view of a galley to show slaves

The picture also gives you a good idea of what the galleys looked like.

John Evelyn, an Englishman who, like Samuel Pepys kept a diary, had visited the French galleys some years earlier; here are his impressions:

> The spectacle was to me new and strange to see so many hundreds of miserably naked persons having their heads shaven close and having onely high red bonnets, a payre of coarse canvas drawers, their whole backs and leggs naked, doubly chayn'd about their middle and leggs, in couples, and made fast to their seates, and all commanded in a *trise* by an *imperious* and cruell seaman. This galley was richly carv'd and gilded and most of the rest were very beautifull.... I was amaz'd to *contemplate* how these miserable *catyfs* lie in their galley crowded together. Their rising forward and falling back at theire oare is a miserable spectacle, and the noyse of their chaines with the roaring of the beaten waters has something of strange and fearfull to one unaccustom'd to it. They are rul'd and chastiz'd by strokes on their backs and soles of their feete

on the least disorder and without the least humanity; yet are they chereful and full of knavery.

Huguenots like Jean Marteilhe joined criminals and Turkish prisoners of war who had also been condemned to the galleys. None escaped the cruel punishments described by Evelyn. Here is Marteilhe's description of the savage way in which a victim would be treated for any real or imagined offence:

> He is extended with his Face downward, his Arms upon one Bench and his Legs upon the Opposite, which are held by two Slaves that stand opposite each other. The Executioner, who is generally a Turkish Slave, stands over him with a Rope in his Hand, with which he is to beat the Criminal without the least mercy; for if he happens to be *remiss*, which is seldom the case, the *sous Comité* uses him as he should have used the Criminal. Thus every stroke is laid on with the Executioner's whole force, so that each Blow raises a *weal* as thick as one's Thumb. Few that are condemned to suffer this Punishment can sustain above ten or twelve Blows without fainting. This, however, does not prevent the Executioner from proceeding.

This punishment, the dreaded 'bastinado', was often given for very small offences and the comité or slave-master would usually order twenty or thirty strokes. Marteilhe had 'seen fifty, eighty or even a hundred ordered; but then, those who are thus punished seldom recover'. After the punishment the victim's back would be rubbed with salt and vinegar which added to his anguish.

Galleys were fighting ships and part of the French navy. Louis XIV was frequently at war and Marteilhe's account shows how much other countries feared and hated fighting against galleys which in calm weather could come upon a sailing ship unawares:

> As a Galley Sails upon such Occasions with prodigious Swiftness, we were soon along side of him (the enemy ship) and with all our Force raised the 'Chamade' or

Shout of the whole Crew, which is done in order to *intimidate* the Enemy. There certainly is something shocking and terrible in the Approach of a Galley. Three hundred Men quite Naked, roaring all at once, and rattling their Chains in the most hideous Manner impresses the Mind with strange Emotions; they must have Hearts well fortified who can sustain the Encounter without trembling.

On this first occasion Marteilhe's galley took a Dutch vessel by surprise and the whole enemy crew were indeed so astonished that they fled into the hold on hearing the dreadful noise and the ship immediately surrendered! Marteilhe was not so lucky when the galley later engaged an English frigate: 'It happened that my Seat on which there were five Frenchmen and one Turk lay just opposite one of the Cannons which I readily perceived was charged. The two Vessels lay so close that by raising my Body in the least, I could touch this Cannon with my Hand.'

Marteilhe watched the English gunner moving from cannon to cannon with a lighted *match* and, saying fervent prayers, prepared himself for death. By some trick of fate the shot passed him although the explosion blew him from his seat as far as the chain would allow. Stunned, he crept back to tell his neighbours that the danger was over but he found he was the only survivor. With this terrible discovery he lost consciousness only to be aroused by an agonising pain caused by a man who had gripped his wounded leg. He discovered he was about to be thrown overboard as dead; there was no burial service for slaves. When Marteilhe cried out that he was alive, he was thrown instead onto a coil of rope in the hold. 'In this suffocating Hole', he wrote, 'the Wounded who might otherwise have survived, died in great Abundance.' Marteilhe recovered, although he was never fit to pull an oar again, and became the captain's secretary instead – a life which he preferred, although he was still, of course, a slave.

In this way Jean Marteilhe suffered for his refusal to give up the Protestant faith, yet strangely enough, his experiences on board ship do not form the most horrifying part of his story. Twelve years after Marteilhe was captured trying to cross the frontier, the English, who had won the great War of the Spanish Succession against Louis XIV, entered Dunkirk, so the French authorities decided to send their Huguenot galley slaves to Marseilles where there was a large fleet, for they feared the Protestant English would want to free them. Thus began for twenty-two Huguenots, the oldest over eighty, a nightmare march across France. In some towns they were welcomed by fellow Protestants or those who had been forced to become Catholics but never forgotten their old faith. This made the authorities even sterner for they feared to lose some of these new converts. At night the slaves would be lodged in prisons, the worst of which was in Paris. Here is Marteilhe's description of this terrible place, the Castle of Tournelle:

> This Prison or rather Cavern is round and of vast Extent. The Floor is made uneven by large Oak Beams which are placed at three Feet Distance from each other. These Beams are two Feet and an half thick. To these are fastened large Iron Chains, a Foot and an half long: At Intervals of two Feet from each other, and at the End of each Chain, is a large Ring of the same Metal. When the Slave is first brought into this Prison, he is made to lie along till his Head touches the Beam; then the Ring is put round his Neck and fastened by an Hammer and Anvil kept for the Purpose. As the Chains are fixed in the Beam at two Feet Distance from each other, and some of the Beams are forty Feet long, twenty Men are thus chained down in a Row; and so in Proportion to the Length of the Beams. In this Manner are fastened five hundred Wretches in an Attitude certainly enough to melt the hardest heart.
>
> Imagine a Man unable to stretch himself along, as the Beam to which his Neck is fixed is too high, and also unable to sit or stand upright, as he is chained down too short; in a Word, the Posture is between sitting and lying; Part of the Body on the Block to which it is chained, and Part on the Floor. We felt Pains beyond Expression in all our limbs, particularly the old Men among us.

After leaving Paris there were many more hardships to be endured. On one occasion the Huguenots and other prisoners were searched for religious books or any other valuables they might have. They were made to take off all their clothes and stand for two hours in frost and wind; even their handkerchiefs were taken away from them. When the order came to move they were too frozen to do so and were beaten and dragged to a stable. Although none of the twenty-two Huguenots died, eighteen other prisoners did that night. The survivors probably owed their lives to the heaps of manure on which they lay for, finding it warm, many of the poor wretches entirely buried themselves in it.

More dead than alive, the procession finally arrived in Marseilles for another *stint* in the galleys, but thanks to a treaty with England, the slaves were freed the following year. Jean Marteilhe and his friends went to Geneva where many people came to meet them and escorted them into the city in a triumphant procession. So after thirteen years Marteilhe was free, but many Huguenots had died through the terrible treatment received in prison and on board the galleys. One can only wonder at the courage that sustained them in their loyalty to their beliefs amidst all their sufferings. Only the bravest Huguenots could undergo what Marteilhe had suffered for his faith. Others were forced to become Catholics and made to go to Mass, but although it has been estimated that 400,000 Huguenots became new converts in this way, many paid only lip service to the Catholic faith and when the worst of the persecution seemed to be over, started to meet together again for psalm-singing. Some Huguenot ministers stayed in France and other secretly returned, so the government brought in the death penalty against them and paid large rewards to anyone who would inform against them.

In spite of everything the government could do, there were some areas of France where Protestants could not be stamped out. One of these was Languedoc where, between 1686 and 1700, there were sixty executions and 320 men condemned to the galleys. Here the governor was now Basville, who had earlier succeeded Marillac in Poitou and whose cruelty was even greater. On one occasion when his soldiers had killed or wounded sixty Protestants and whipped the survivors with stirrup straps, Basville congratulated the captain responsible, saying that his only regret was that he had not cut off all the women's noses!

Faced with the dragonnades, violence and torture ordered by this tyrant, the people of Languedoc were driven to rebellion. When their churches were destroyed and their ministers sent abroad, the Protestants met in secret and some young men and women became unofficial preachers. A few of them even claimed the gift of prophecy and soon inspired the simple country people to religious frenzy. Lacking churches they would meet in some wild lonely place like the one in the picture. Thus the 'Church of the Desert' was born. The

The Church of the Desert

Rebels in the Cévennes 1703   *Jean Cavalier*

Camisard revolt, as it was called, broke out in 1702. The rebels, already much excited by religious 'prophesyings', also felt strongly about heavy taxation, so they hanged tax collectors and massacred priests, shouting, 'No taxes and religious liberty!' The government reacted savagely and any rebels caught were broken on the wheel. Soldiers were sent to put down the revolt, but as Louis was at war with England and other countries he had few spare troops, and because of this and because the rocks, caves and woods of Languedoc offered such good hideouts, the rebels held out for two years.

The hero of this unpleasant little war, in the mountain region known as the Cévennes, was Jean Cavalier, a kind of Robin Hood who plundered Catholics to provide food and necessities for his outlawed Protestant followers. A man who had met him wrote this description:

He was a slight, fair man, with a pleasant and *refined* expression. Among his followers he was known as David. From baker's apprentice he became at the age of twenty-three the leader of a fairly large body of followers, owing to his courage and with the help of a prophetess who declared that he was appointed by *express* command of the Holy Ghost. He was at the head of 800 men whom he was forming into regiments.

77

The Camisards, so called because of the 'chemises' or shirts they wore over their other clothes, gave so much trouble to the French army that they were offered a truce, for they could not be defeated. Thus 'the great monarch' Louis XIV made peace with a baker's apprentice! Cavalier even paid a visit to Louis's wonderful palace at Versailles, where the king saw him but did not speak to him, perhaps not surprisingly. Soon, however, Cavalier began to fear that his life would be in danger if he stayed in Catholic France, so he fled and joined the king's enemies, ending up as a general in the English army and governor of the island of Jersey. Few men can have had a stranger career.

After Cavalier left the Cévennes the revolt broke out again, but at the end of a long struggle the government discovered the rebels' plans and hiding places and those who did not manage to flee abroad were crushed. Yet by the time Louis XIV's long reign ended in 1715, the Church of the Desert had made steady progress and in spite of all the persecution the Huguenot spirit was still unbroken in many parts of France.

9 Dispersion

In spite of the risks, thousands of Huguenots succeeded in leaving France, both before and after the Revocation of the Edict of Nantes. The first part of this chapter tells the story of one refugee, Jacques Fontaine, who wrote his memoirs nearly forty years later. His book helps us to understand the difficulties faced by the Huguenots, not only in leaving France, but in trying to make a home in another country. 'At last the great persecutor Louis XIV, having broken and revoked the Edict of Nantes, the month of October 1685, I saw that I must perish or leave', wrote Fontaine. With his fiancée Anne-Elisabeth Boursiquot, 'the only blonde of all her family, and a real beauty', her younger sister and his niece Jeannette, he waited on a beach with fifty or sixty other refugees for a ship. Like Jean Migault he was not lucky the first time and had to return to a nearby town.

Four or five days later Fontaine heard that he must take his party in an open boat and transfer to an English ship a little way out at sea. Two young men and another six girls joined them in the hired boat and all went well until they were about to signal the English ship by lowering and raising their sail three times as agreed beforehand. Suddenly a French *frigate* appeared, and anchoring alongside the English ship, sent a search party on board. Finding no Protestants, the French told the captain to set sail. The *fugitives* in the open boat were in a terrible fright lest they should be left behind or discovered, or both. Then Fontaine had an idea which the boatman and his son agreed to carry out. Covering the refugees in the bottom of the boat with an old sail, they boldly sailed right up to the frigate pretending to be drunk and to have lost their way. In their drunken quarrel one let the sail down, apparently by mistake. The other raised it, then dropped it in his turn and it fell once again before they got it up. Thus the English captain knew that he must wait a while and the frigate's crew advised the drunken fools (as they thought) to turn back, for they would never get into port in that condition. So the small boat put out to sea in the *wake* of the English ship and the frigate sailed away unsuspecting. In a little while the refugees were on their way to England. 'Happy day I say, for us who had run so many risks', wrote Fontaine years afterwards.

The party was eleven days at sea before arriving weary, hungry and almost entirely without possessions

at Appledore in the Bristol Channel at the mouth of the little river that passes through Barnstaple, 1st December

Barnstaple in the early eighteenth century

1685. But God who had not brought us to a safe country to have us die of starvation, touched the hearts of the principal inhabitants of Barnstaple who, having sent to find us, all twelve, each took one of us into his house and treated us with unbelievable kindness and friendship, each one taking such care of the Frenchman or French-woman whom he had in his house, that we might have been their own children or their brothers, and thus God let us find among strangers, fathers, mothers, brothers and sisters.

English people on the whole welcomed their fellow Protestants with generosity, and collections made for them totalled many thousands of pounds throughout the country. But understandably, the Huguenots did not wish to live on charity and, like Jacques Fontaine, wanted to start in busi-ness. 'I must recall, with thanks to God for his *providence*, the first mouthful of bread that I ate on arrival at Appledore', he wrote. Fontaine noticed that biscuits 'as big as plates' which were brought to him cost only a quarter of the French price. Soon he went into business with his English host, a Mr Downe, and sent a cargo of wheat to people he knew in France. They sent back wine and a good profit was made. Unfortunately the next three cargoes made a loss, due to dishonesty at the other end so Fontaine had to give up. Mean-while a rather comic thing happened. Mr Downe's sister had fallen in love with Jacques Fontaine, so she persuaded her brother to propose to Fontaine's fiancée, Anne, so that she herself might marry Fontaine. The latter, however, escaped by pretending he knew very little English, and quickly married his sweetheart. The people of Barnstaple appear to have taken the young couple to their hearts for they came to see their small house and, as Fontaine said,

> having been told of my poverty, furnished it with every-thing necessary for a little home in the most generous manner in the world so that I saw my house furnished without it costing me a farthing. But that was not all, for on market days grain, meat and poultry were given in abundance without my knowing to whom I was obliged.

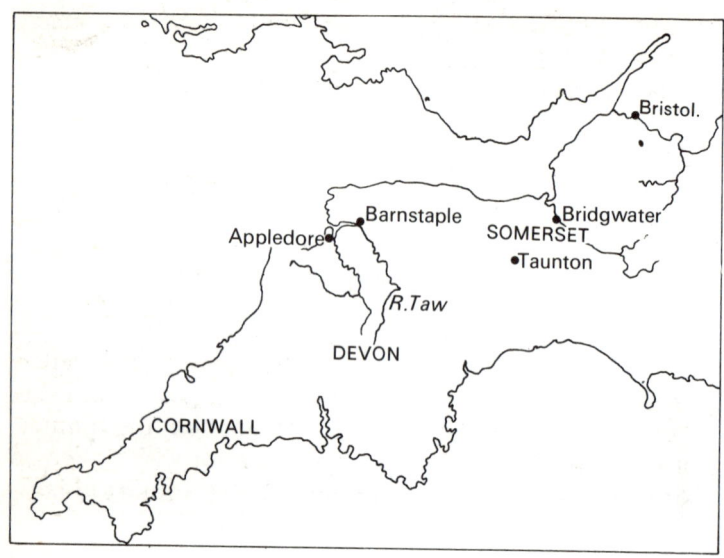

West Country towns connected with Jacques Fontaine

Fontaine stayed in Barnstaple for a year but was still anxious to live by his own work and not by charity. After a short time at Bridgwater he settled in Taunton where he started to make cloth and also opened a shop. His methods were more up to date than those of manufacturers and shop-keepers in the town and he began to do well. His competitors were jealous and tried to ruin him by bringing him before the mayor's court; but a clever lawyer asked his opponents whether they would prefer to keep Fontaine and his family from the rates or have him earn a living. Fontaine was acquitted but was never free from jealous opposition while he remained in Taunton. By 1694 he had made £1,000 and decided to try his fortune elsewhere. He had now become a minister and was hoping to start a French church and open a school wherever he should settle. He also packed the tools he would need if he decided to take up cloth manufacture again. It took twelve horses to get his possessions to Bristol. From there he set sail for Cork in southern Ireland.

Many Huguenots chose Ireland for, ever since 1662, the *viceroys* had promised every advantage to French refugees

William of Orange

who would establish wool or silk manufacture there. Provided they took an oath of *allegiance* to the king of England they were considered as 'natural born and faithful subjects of His Majesty'. This allowed them to set up their trades and industries with fewer restrictions than in England where they were still treated as foreigners. When William of Orange became king in 1689 he encouraged the linen industry and personally invited a Huguenot, Louis Crommelin, then living in Holland, to settle in Ireland and establish his industry on a firm basis. Crommelin had learnt how to make linen from his father in France the home of the finest linen at that time, and had perfected his craft in Holland where they made the whitest. In addition to his professional skills, Crommelin had tact, generosity, inexhaustible energy and complete honesty. He knew how to attract and keep workers and soon had, as well as the experienced Dutch and French craftsmen he had brought with him, hundreds of Irish employed at Lisburn near Belfast. Before Crommelin's arrival in 1698 only about 300,000 yards of linen were exported in a year, but in 1710, 1,688,574 yards were sent abroad. By 1796 the total was

47,000,000 yards, and the Irish linen industry still flourishes today.

In Cork, Jacques Fontaine was soon engaged in the manufacture of woollen cloth and he took care also to set up the French church he had planned. A large room on the first floor of Fontaine's house was used for services. He had it furnished with benches for the congregation and a pulpit for his preaching. But soon a jealous rival in business made trouble for Fontaine in his congregation and when the English parliament forbade, through fear of competition, the export of Irish cloth, Fontaine was again ruined. He decided to take up fishing and moved to a lonely spot called Bearhaven on the south-west coast of Ireland, but the first year there were few fish, and the next year his partners were using the boats for trade with Spain, so he had little luck. By this time he was farming as well and had built himself a stone house.

England and France were now at war again and he was forced to fortify his home against French pirate crews who would land on that coast to burn and plunder the farms. The first time this happened Fontaine skilfully defended his house watched by two or three hundred Irish who, being Catholics, were waiting for a share of the loot. After an eight-hour defence, Fontaine's powder was running short, but he had killed three of the enemy and wounded seven, while only one of his dozen or so men had been wounded. At the critical moment the enemy retreated and later a grateful government awarded Fontaine a pension of five shillings a day for having helped to defend the coast in wartime. Four years later, however, when another pirate crew landed, Fontaine was not so successful, as he had only his own family at home. They made a fight of it but finally surrendered on promise of their lives, and had to watch their house being destroyed and their possessions carried off. In spite of the promise, Fontaine, who was wounded, was taken on board the pirate ship until £100 ransom could be raised. Next day his wife borrowed £30, on receipt of which the pirates released Fontaine but took one of his sons instead. When the government heard of this, all French prisoners in Irish and English ports were clapped into *irons* and so great was the fuss that the lad, Pierre, was freed without further payment.

In compensation for his losses Fontaine was awarded £800 by the government, so he bought a house in Dublin. It was said to be haunted but, as a good Huguenot, he did not believe in ghosts and was pleased to get it cheap. The 'ghosts' turned out to be a band of beggars living in the empty house. Fontaine soon dealt with them. Then at long last he was able to set up the school he had dreamed of and also educate his own family. By the time their father died in 1722 or 1723, most of Fontaine's sons and daughters had gone to Virginia to make yet another start, and there their families flourished. It was a great-grand-daughter in America who discovered Jacques Fontaine's manuscript and had it published, and from this we know the story of his life.

Fontaine's children were among many Huguenots who went to America to seek freedom and fortune. Some went to New York by way of England or Holland and others founded towns of their own like New Rochelle near Long Island Sound. As the name suggests most of the early settlers came from the neighbourhood of La Rochelle. It was some time before Huguenots in the New World could settle to their usual occupations but most of them were able to live comfortably.

Other Huguenots to travel far from their native France were those who left Holland to go to the Cape of Good Hope, then a Dutch colony. The next picture shows the settlement at Fransche Hoek or French Corner at the foot of the Drakenstein Mountains. The settlers were given as much land as they could cultivate and encouraged to plant vines and olives. Although only a small number of Huguenots went to such a completely unknown country they formed about one seventh of the European population there. One family, called de Villiers, came from near La Rochelle where three brothers, Pierre, Abraham and Jacob had worked on a farm. They had to leave their youngest brother behind as he was too young to travel. They set out from Holland in a ship called the 'Zion' and had a difficult journey with much illness on board. They cheered themselves and kept up their

85

courage by prayers every morning and evening, and every Huguenot had a Bible in French or a book of French psalms. The three brothers laid out a farm in Fransche Hoek and called it La Rochelle; they bought a horse so that they could ride to church in a nearby town. They all married Huguenot girls and Pierre made his home at the original farm which is still there with an oak tree planted by him. He had twenty-five children and lived to see his hundredth grandchild. No wonder the name de Villiers became well known in South Africa! First one and then another of Pierre's descendants became Chief Justice, but by that time there was nothing but their names to distinguish Huguenot from Dutch settlers, as the French language soon died out and with it the need for separate French churches.

It is rare nowadays to find a surviving Huguenot settlement where French is spoken, but a kind of French is still used at Friedrichsdorf in Germany. It was originally known as Das Neue Dorf (the new village) and was partly built by refugees from many parts of France. The ruler of that part of Germany, Frederick II of Hesse-Homburg, allowed the settlers freedom from taxation for a period of ten years, land without interest, meadows for their cattle, a form of self-government and the right to establish industries. The settlement flourished and its chief industry became the making of Zweibäcke (biscuits) which have been exported to all parts of the world. Other German princes too were generous to French refugees, for they knew that their own industries and trade would benefit. Brandenburg-Prussia under a famous *Elector* called Frederick William offered them ships and provisions to travel to ports like Hamburg and from there they were taken to cities throughout his lands. Agricultural labourers were particularly welcome; so were paper-makers, glassmakers and other craftsmen. Ten thousand Huguenots settled in Berlin which, before their coming, was a mean, poor sort of place; but the crafts and trades brought by the Huguenots set it on its way to become a great European capital. Frederick William also welcomed Huguenots into his army and to centres of learning where they made a contribution to science and literature.

Fransche Hoek (French Corner) in South Africa

South African farm owned by the de Villiers

Amsterdam, by Ruisdael

The greatest centre of refuge for the Huguenots was Holland. It has been estimated that as many as 75,000 settled there and that about one fifth of them went to the great commercial city of Amsterdam where they were freed from taxes for twelve years. As in Ireland, the new arrivals could be naturalised and receive full citizenship, although in Holland, these privileges were granted a little later. Many Huguenot refugees offered their services to the Dutch ruler, William of Orange, who was leading Europe in the wars against Louis XIV. It is believed that altogether 9,000 sailors, 600 army officers and 12,000 valuable troops were lost by France and

gained by her enemies. Once Huguenots changed sides to fight against their persecutor, they remained, with very few exceptions, loyal to their new masters. When Jacques Fontaine's son Pierre was held hostage on board the pirate ship the French crew invited him to help them against the English, but he replied that if he took up arms at all, he would turn against his captors instead, for, he declared, the English were his nation and his friends. In these years Louis XIV lost, and his enemies gained, not only the loyalty of one boy, but the services and skills of thousands of those who had been his subjects.

10 *Huguenots in England*

Registers of baptisms, marriages and deaths kept in many of their churches help us to trace the history of the Huguenots' settlements in England. Many came to London where they had churches of their own as early as the sixteenth century. The best known Huguenot church was in Threadneedle Street in the City of London; it was rebuilt after the great fire in 1666 and became the central place of worship for French Protestants.

Close to the church in Threadneedle Street was a mansion where Sir John Houblon lived with his wife Marie. He was the grandson of an early Huguenot refugee and was a British subject. He was rich and successful and became Lord Mayor of London in 1695. The year before, he had subscribed £10,000 towards the Bank of England when it was founded to raise money to help William of Orange fight Louis XIV. Houblon became the Bank's first governor. Seven of the twenty-four founder-directors were also descendants of Huguenots who, like the French soldiers and sailors fighting for William, wanted to see Louis defeated. You probably know that the Bank of England is sometimes called 'The Old Lady of Threadneedle Street' and it was on the site of Houblon's house that the Bank was built in the eighteenth century. The first governor of the Bank of Ireland was also a Huguenot.

Not only did Huguenots act as Britain's bankers, they printed her banknotes too. This was done by the Portal family who were–and are–paper manufacturers in Hampshire. They suffered the full horrors of the dragonnade while in France, for, when they fled, they were discovered and the

Portal's paper mill in Hampshire, founded 1712

mother, father and one of the children were killed. The remaining four children hid in a great bread oven and were saved. They made their way to the coast, reached Bordeaux where they were able to get a passage on a merchant ship bound for Holland and escaped, hidden this time in barrels. Henri and Guillaume de Portal served William of Orange and came with him to England where Henri set up a paper mill. Their paper was so fine and white in contrast to the coarse brown stuff which had been used until then that when the directors of the Bank wanted banknotes printed they naturally turned to Portals to make the special paper needed. The firm is still making it today.

Huguenots were to be found in almost every industry, art and craft. A designer, Daniel Marot, started a new fashion in chairs and introduced blue and white Delft china in the Dutch style but with his own patterns. Huguenots brought the skills of tapestry and carpet weaving to England and made silk at Spitalfields in London. They were skilled in everything to do with cloth manufacture. Refugees, both before and after the Revocation, brought with them the secrets of glassmaking, clockmaking, and silk stocking and felt manufacture. Some were skilled in metal crafts, like

Chair designed by Daniel Marot

Coffee pot made by Paul de Lamerie

Paul de Lamerie, a famous silversmith who made the elegant coffee pot shown in the picture. Huguenots took part in many other trades from soap boiling to the brewing of vinegar. In fact as one writer put it:

> There was scarcely a branch of trade in Great Britain but at once felt the beneficial effects of the large *influx* of experienced workmen from France. Besides improving those manufactures which had already been established, they introduced many entirely new branches of industry; and by their skill, their intelligence and their laboriousness, they richly repaid England for the hospitality and the *asylum* which had been so generously extended to them in their time of need.

What made the Huguenot contribution twice as valuable was that everything England gained was also lost to Louis XIV.

The map shows the main Huguenot settlements in England. The largest early ones were at Canterbury, Nor-

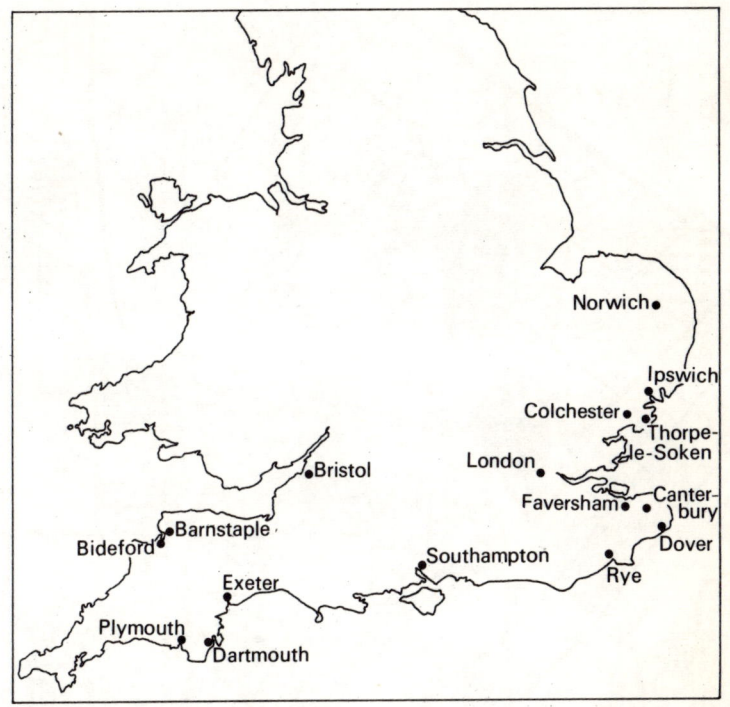

Places with Huguenot churches in 1700

wich and Southampton. After the Revocation more refugees came, especially to Colchester, Exeter, Plymouth and Bristol. To see how the newcomers lived, worked and worshipped, and how their English neighbours reacted to them, we shall look more closely at the Bristol refuge.

Huguenot refugees coming to Bristol by sea sailed up the Bristol Channel, then on the tide up the river Avon and through the famous Clifton Gorge. Soon they had their first glimpse of the city, with the towers and spires of its seventeen churches silhouetted against the sky. Their ship probably then turned into the river Froome to deposit goods and passengers on the main quay at St Augustine's Back, which you can see on page 94 on the map of Bristol made in 1673. John Evelyn the diarist, visiting the city some years earlier, wrote:

Part of a map of Bristol made in 1673

Went to Bristoll, a City *emulating* London, not for its large extent, but manner of building, shops, bridge, traffiq, market place etc... The City wholly *mercantile* as standing neere the famous Severne, *commodiously* for Ireland and the Western world. Here I first saw the manner of refining suggar.

The map of Bristol referred to was made by James Millerd 'citizen and inhabitant there'. All round the edge were pictures like this one of the bridge over the Avon which Millerd described as 'a very faire and loftie stone Bridge, built on either side with houses and shopps which, though in length it cometh much short of, yet in fairnesse of buildings goeth as much beyond the famous Bridge of London over Thames'.

Bristol bridge

Bristoll Bridg over Avon flu.

Millerd and Evelyn were two people who compared Bristol with London, but to the Huguenots, few of whom knew London, Bristol seemed most to resemble La Rochelle. Both faced westwards for trade with the New World. Ocean-going ships could come right into the centre of both cities, so in both there was a community of merchants, seamen and shipbuilders. Industries were similar; for instance, cloth-making was as important in Bristol as in La Rochelle. Most Huguenots found jobs quickly and the news of opportunities attracted others. Thus the Bristol refuge grew, and by 1705 there were at least 324 Huguenot families there. Not sur-prisingly, a very high proportion, about 80 per cent, came from the west coast of France, from La Rochelle and the provinces of Saintonge, Aunis and Poitou nearby.

Although the occupations of all the Huguenots in Bristol are not known, the following table for the 149 that are, will give you a good idea of the kind of people who came to Bristol:

Weavers	50 (32.2%)	Tiler	1 (0.6%)
Sailors	47 (31%)	Joiner	1
Merchants	15 (9.8%)	Labourer	1
Tailors	7 (4.7%)	Locksmith	1
Doctors of medicine	4 (2.6%)	Landowner	1
Leatherworkers	3 (2%)	Farm labourer	1
Hatters	3	Clockmaker	1
Pastors	3	Student	1
Goldsmiths	2 (1.3%)	Button maker	1
Shoemakers	2	Wig maker	1
Coopers	2	Halberdier	1

It is likely that nearly all these people found similar employ-ment in Bristol.

Sea-borne trade was the source of most of Bristol's wealth. Here is a list of countries or ports visited by 265 vessels which brought cargoes to the port in 1678–79, with the number of vessels visiting each one:

Ireland	77	Portugal	6
West Indies	50	Hamburg	4

America	28	Stockholm	3
Spain	25	Newfoundland	3
Rotterdam	16	Zante	2
France	15	Madeira	2
Scotland	8	Other ports	18
Norway	8		

From this information you can work out the chief imports of the city. Ireland sent the raw materials for three of Bristol's principal industries: soap, leather and wool. From the West Indies came sugar, and from America, tobacco. Both Evelyn and his fellow diarist Pepys wrote about the excellent Spanish wine they enjoyed in the city, Pepys referring to it as 'Bristol Milk', by which name the sherry is still known today. All sorts of goods came from Holland and France; a ship arriving from La Rochelle in 1650 was 'laden with salt, vinegar, prewens (prunes), *lees* of wine, and paper with other small goods and *commodities*'. In exchange Bristol ships took out cargoes of butter and other farm produce from the West of England, or coal which was mined not far away.

Rich Huguenot merchants, if they had managed to bring their money out of France, were soon venturing their capital in ships and cargoes, and in a short time three or four Huguenot families were among the richest in the city. As early as 1693 Etienne Peloquin, the senior Huguenot merchant, was given the freedom of the city by the mayor which shows the high *esteem* in which the French community was already held by most people. Etienne's grandson David, born in 1699, became Lord Mayor of Bristol in 1751 and died in 1766, leaving a fortune of £80,000 to his half-sister Marie-Anne. It is interesting to know that when Marie-Anne died a few years later, she left £19,000 to found a charity for the Bristol poor. Interest on this sum provided, among other things, about £6 each every year for thirty-eight poor men and thirty-eight poor women of Bristol. £6 would be three or four months' wages for a poor man in those days. Today the money is invested in a building which has recently been modernised and converted into an office block called Peloquin Chambers. This is situated in St Augustine's Parade, on the very spot where most of the French refugees first landed and is a reminder of the history of the Huguenots in the town. From the rents and other profits the Peloquin charity is still regularly distributed, and some of the money is also used for scholarships and grants at Bristol Grammar School. Thus the charity extended to the Huguenots in their need has been, and is still being, amply repaid.

In the eighteenth century another family, the Laroches, became as rich and well known in Bristol as the Peloquins. Here is the family tree:

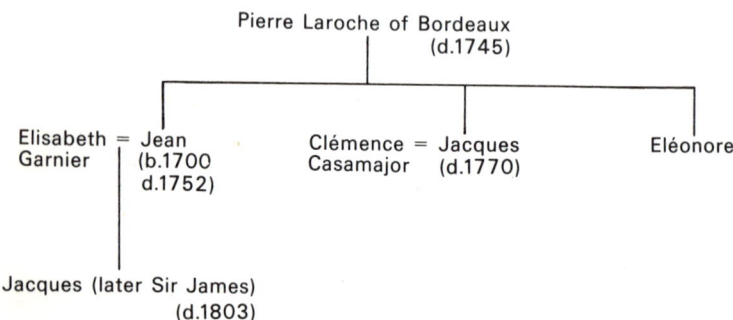

The children of Pierre Laroche were born in England. Jean married well and became a Member of Parliament while Jacques made an equally good marriage to the daughter of another rich Huguenot merchant, and before 1731 had set up in business himself, importing goods from Jamaica. He became noted for his activities in the war against Spain which broke out in 1739 when he fitted out, with others, a vessel, the 'Queen Mary' of 200 tons with 20 cannon and a crew of fifty to prey on enemy shipping. During the course of the war ninety-six such pirate vessels were armed at Bristol, Jacques Laroche having shares in at least ten of them. Here is an advertisement from the 'Bristol Oracle' of September 1744, giving details of the 'Resolution', one of the ships in which Laroche had an interest. By 1744 Britain was at war with France as well and Laroche and his partners must have made a fortune from the voyage of one of their privateers, the 'Southwell', that year and the next, for she took eleven

BRISTOL, Sept. 18, 1744.

ON A

CRUIZE

And will Sail in a very short Time,

The RESOLUTION *Privateer*,

Capt. *Thomas Elworthy*, Commander,

Burthen 200 Tons, a prime Sailer, mounts 16 Carriage Guns 6 Pounders, 20 Swivels, and 160 Men.

ALL Gentlemen Sailors, willing to serve on board the said Ship, now lying in the Dock, near the great Crane, may apply to the Captain, on board, where they shall have all proper Encouragement; or, at Mr. *James Ward*'s, at the *Lamb* and *Flag* on the Key, near the *Merchant's-Hall*, which is the Place of Rendezvous.

enemy vessels in a voyage lasting nineteen months. Before that, the same ship took eight prizes in five weeks! On her last voyage as a privateer the 'Southwell' did less well; her one prize, divided amongst the shareholders, brought Jacques Laroche only £11 16s 3d in return for his expenditure of £157 6s 5½d! The partners now decided to use the vessel in the slave trade instead.

Both Jacques Laroche and his nephew of the same name whom he took into partnership, had extensive interests in the slave trade; no one had yet protested against this terrible traffic. In later years when the subject was under discussion in Parliament, the younger Jacques Laroche, by this time an M.P. like his father, spoke strongly for the rights of merchants in the trade. No doubt he and his uncle had made much money out of it, starting with the voyage of the 'Southwell' in 1746 when 301 slaves were landed in the West Indies to face a life of unending toil on the plantations, growing the sugar

Houses in Queen Square Bristol

that helped to make Bristol rich. If Jacques Laroche senior who had shares in this venture cared about the death of 150 other Negroes on the voyage, it was probably only because of the amount of profit he lost.

The proceeds of privateering and the slave trade enabled the Laroche family to lead a comfortable life. Like other rich Bristol merchants, they lived in the new and fashionable Queen Square area, with their grand houses full of fine walnut furniture, costly hangings, mirrors and silverware. Their cellars were full of port wine and the best 'Bristol Milk', and, although they worked hard, they lived elegantly. It must not be thought, however, that these families were typical of the Bristol Huguenots. Many, like sea captains, owners of workshops, lawyers and others were comfortably off, but in contrast, a working man's wage would be twenty-five shillings a month, or up to fifty-five shillings for a skilled man. Some old and sick people and widows with young children had to be helped from a charity known as the Royal Bounty from which Bristol got first £12 and later £18 a year. The Bristol Huguenots therefore had their very rich and their very poor members, like any other community. As usually happens, there were more poor than rich, which worried the city council, especially when the refugees first arrived. 'Give us full directions how to dispose of those French already come', wrote the Mayor to a government minister in London

in 1681. In 1693 the M.P. for Bristol made a speech against the 'Froglanders' as he called them and finished by calling for the foreigners to be kicked out of the kingdom. From this you can see that not everyone welcomed the Huguenots, for many grudged charity to the poor and resented the rich.

Until they learned English and became a part of Bristol society, the Huguenots had their own church in the city. If you look back at the map at the beginning of the chapter you will see opposite College Green a building called the Gaunts, another name for the chapel of St Mark which belonged to the city corporation. Through the interest of Bishop Trelawny of Bristol, the Huguenots were able to worship there from 1687 until 1720 when the corporation wanted it back. Then the Huguenots built a chapel of their own in Orchard Street which served them until the death of their last pastor, Pierre Gautier, in 1791. The congregation was officially dissolved in 1814 as the need for it had passed and the Huguenots differed only in their names from Bristolians.

The Huguenots did not greatly change Bristol, but they added to it and played a part in its development. There is little doubt that without the skill and resource of the hard-working sober French Protestant communities which finally became a part of them, many English towns would be poorer today.

11 Conclusion

In 1685 when the Huguenot church at La Rochelle was destroyed, the church bell had to become Catholic. First it was whipped for having used its voice to call Protestants to worship, and buried in the earth to mark the end of its sinful life. Then it was symbolically reborn by being dug up again, two Catholics attending the ceremony in the roles of mid-wife and wet-nurse! After that the bell was baptised and handed over to a neighbouring Catholic parish. It was now a 'new convert', as the Catholics hoped all Huguenots left in France would become. To encourage them they were given certain privileges like exemption from paying their debts for three years. So, when called upon to pay for the bell, its new owners claimed the same exemption for it and said no payment would be made until the time was up.

Persecution made many new converts, but most of them never became convinced Catholics, and the Church lost respect and influence because of this. Some, although forced to say they were Catholics, remained secret Protestants, like a couple called Jean and Marie Court who lived in a little mountain village in Languedoc in the south of France. Their son Antoine was born there in 1695 and baptised in the Catholic Church because his parents did not dare refuse. His father died when Antoine was very young and his mother brought him up as a secret Protestant. Soon he began attending with her the meetings of the 'Church of the Desert'. When he grew up Antoine became a preacher himself but soon realised that there were weaknesses in the Church he served. Worst of all was the lack of trained pastors so that so-called prophets and prophetesses were gaining influence instead. Court feared the spread of ignorance and superstition and decided to build up again the organisation and discipline that Calvin had given the Church. He soon made others see his point of view and the prophets and prophetesses gradually disappeared. Court had Protestant books, particularly Bibles, distributed to instruct the people, and in 1720 went to Geneva for two years to improve his own knowledge and to interest others there in the work he was trying to do in France.

Court spent some years after this travelling around France preaching and re-establishing Protestant organisation in the districts he visited. Everything had to be done in secret and often his life was in danger, for all pastors who were captured were put to death. Once he was writing a sermon beneath a tree when a band of soldiers appeared in the distance. Court quickly climbed the tree! On another occasion the house where he was staying was searched. His host pretended to be ill and out of respect for the 'sick' man the soldiers did not approach his bed, never guessing that the Protestant minister they sought was hidden behind it. By his work Court saved and strengthened the Church of the Desert and many new congregations were formed. There was such a shortage of pastors for these that in 1726 Court left France and opened a college in Lausanne in Switzerland to train young men for the ministry. Here they gained not only knowledge but also the spiritual strength to enable them to face death for their faith.

One of Court's pupils took up his duties in Normandy where he was joyfully welcomed by a congregation that had been without a pastor for many years. The hard work and constant danger affected the young man's health, however, and he was forced to flee to Jersey. We next hear of him in Bristol, for he was Pierre Gautier who became minister to the Huguenot congregation there in 1758. He never forgot his old teacher Antoine Court and wrote to him, and then to his son who carried on his work, for many years. Four years before Gautier's death and only two before the great revolution of 1789, persecution came to an end in France, for ideas had been changing and it was agreed that Protestants could not be denied certain 'natural' rights, which was a way of saying they could hold religious assemblies again. So Antoine Court and his son had not worked in vain for, thanks to them, there were still Protestants left in France to enjoy their freedom. Yet the Huguenots abroad did not return, for they had become a part of the communities in which they now lived. Even Gautier, who had worked in France, did not go back but served his tiny congregation in Bristol until he died there in 1791.

So the persecution ended and today we can look back not only with horror and grief at what happened to the Huguenots, but with admiration for their achievements. Jean Calvin, who was in many ways the most able religious leader of his time, may be said to be their founder; in Coligny they produced a military leader who was also a man of noble character; in Henry IV perhaps the greatest of French kings and in his minister Sully a statesman of genius. Bernard Palissy was an outstanding artist and craftsman, and Agrippa d'Aubigné a great French poet. Antoine Court's courage and leadership in the face of tremendous hardships deserve to be mentioned and so too do the deeds of many ordinary people. We know of Jean Migault, Jacques Fontaine and Jean Marteilhe from their memoirs and diaries, but there were thousands of others who met their troubles with equal *fortitude* and many, like the pastor Philibert Hamelin, who suffered death rather than give up their faith. Skilled and hard-working, the Huguenots who left France had much to offer their new countries and in many lands they are remembered with gratitude today, particularly by those who can proudly say, 'My ancestors were Huguenots'.

Things To Do

1 Trace or copy a large map of France onto cardboard. Name and colour all the provinces and the chief towns as shown on the map on p. 5. Cut it up and make a jigsaw puzzle with each province as one piece.

2 Draw or make a cut-out silhouette of the 'strange procession' described in chapter 1.

3 Make a list of all the churches in your town or area. Look inside as many as you can. Which most resembles the Huguenot temple at Lyons (p. 11 and which least resembles it? Why?

4 Hold or write a discussion in which one side attacks and the other defends the massacre of St Bartholomew's Day. Can you compare the situation with any in the world today?

5 Write out the conversation (and act it with a friend) between Bernard Palissy and his wife when he comes in tired out at night after another unsuccessful attempt which has involved burning some of the floor-boards (see page 38).

6 Do you agree with Agrippa d'Aubigné about the things which make life worthwhile (see page 48)? What would you cut out of his list and what would you add? Can you explain why your ideas are different from, or largely the same as, his?

7 Imagine yourself a Huguenot citizen of La Rochelle during the great siege. You take a vital interest in all that is going on inside the city and gather what news you can from outside. Each month or so you write a brief entry in your 'siege diary' to show what has happened or how you are feeling. Reproduce these entries.

8 Study the picture of a seventeenth-century schoolroom and the words below it, on page 59. List the similarities and differences between this schoolroom and your own. Which list is longer? Are you surprised?

9 Write a conversation between two Catholic neighbours of Huguenots who are being persecuted. One Catholic believes

that any methods are justified to achieve God's work, the other is horrified at what is going on. A Huguenot woman and child come running out of their house in the greatest distress . . . Act your dialogue or read it for a tape recording.

10 From the description and the picture in chapter 8 make a model or a scale diagram of a galley.

11 From the description in chapter 8 make a model of the prison floor in the Castle of Tournelle. With dolls or cut-out figures show how prisoners were chained down.

12 Write an imaginary conversation between Jacques Fontaine, saying why he intends to leave England, and a Bristol Huguenot who prefers to stay (see chapters 9 and 10).

13 Find out all you can about any Huguenot settlements in your area. Is there any visible reminder of them in the town, or are any of their descendants still to be found?

How Do We Know?

Much of the information in this book is to be found in general histories of France by both English and French writers. 'The Age of Louis XIV' by Voltaire, the famous French philosopher and scholar, has been used and, among others, 'The Sun King' by Nancy Mitford, a beautifully illustrated book which you would probably find interesting. We have also used, as most historians do, letters, journals, diaries and books written by people of the time. Bernard Palissy for instance, wrote a great deal, not only about pottery making but about his own life and ideas, and it is through him that we know about Philibert Hamelin and the early Protestants of Saintes. The memoirs of important people like the Duke of Sully help us with national history, while others like Jean Migault show us how ordinary folk were faring. Pictures and engravings are an obvious source of information, and examples of the skilled craftsmanship of the Huguenots can also be seen in museums and other collections. Tapestries, silverware, furniture and clocks are among the things to look for. Some of the houses of the Huguenots are still standing, such as the Huguenot weavers' house in Canterbury where the looms too are preserved. In France you can visit places like La Rochelle where there are many reminders of the Huguenots, not least in the city Archives, a collection of records and documents concerning the history of the port. Bristol too has its Archives where information was gathered from Apprentice Lists, Poll Books, Poor Books, Rent Books and so on. Then there are the Registers kept by the Huguenot churches in England. These have been studied very carefully by scholars, particularly the Fellows, as they are called, of the Huguenot Society of London which has published many articles and longer studies on the history of the Huguenots both in France and in the countries where they settled. The Society has an excellent library containing books and documents connected with the Huguenots. These are frequently consulted by people wishing to know something about their Huguenot ancestors. The Huguenot Society has members throughout the world.

Glossary

all in, (here means) exhausted
allegiance, loyalty, faithfulness
to annihilate, to destroy completely
apex, tip
ardent, burning, eager
arquebus, old-fashioned hand gun
arrears, unpaid debts
asylum, shelter, refuge
austere, strict, self-disciplined
banned, forbidden
to billet, tó lodge by order
to breach, to make an opening in
bureau, office
bull, Pope's letter
canticle, sacred song or chant
Cardinal, highest rank under Pope in the Catholic Church
catyf (or *caitiff*), wretch
cavalry, horse soldiers
château, French for castle, large country house
chrysalis, insect larva inside its *cocoon*
cocoon, silken wrapping spun by larva (caterpillar) before it turns
    into an insect
comité, slave master on a galley; *sous comité,* his second in command
commodiously, conveniently
commodity, article traded
composure, (have) calmness
to concoct, to boil together
confessor, priest who hears sins confessed
congenial, like-minded
to contemplate, to gaze upon
convert, person who changes his religion
to convert, to change a person's religion

credit side, right, or profit, side

dearth, scarcity

to despoil, to rob

destitute, entirely without anything

devout, strongly religious

diadem, crown

dragoon, soldier, usually horse-mounted

eccentric, odd

effigy, image

elder (of a church), senior member of congregation

Elector, German prince with right to vote in elections for the emperor

to emulate, to copy

to encumber, to burden

esteem, regard, good opinion

express, direct, clear

fatigue, tiredness

figuline, article made of potter's clay

fluted, grooved

fortitude, courage

frigate, small warship

fugitive, one who flees

galley, (here) warship propelled by oars

glaze, shiny surface of pottery

halberd, axelike weapon, wielded by a halberdier

hulk, hull or body of an old ship

immorality, wickedness

imperious, haughty, commanding

importunity, tiresome request or command

infantry, foot soldiers

influx, flowing in

ingredient, one item in a mixture

to intimidate, to frighten

intolerable, unbearable

intricate, complicated

irons, (here) fetters, ring and chain to hold a prisoner

lees, dregs

legitimate, lawful

livre, old French coin

majority, group having the greater number of members

mantle, cloak

Mass, Catholic communion service

massacre, wholesale killing of one group of people by another

match, (here) slow-burning rope used to fire guns
mercantile, commercial
mercenary, hired foreign soldier
minority, inferior number, opposite of *majority*
mizen (mizzen) mast, mast at prow of galley (on later ships at stern)
musket, old-fashioned hand gun, larger than an *arquebus*
obese, fat
ominous, threatening
ordinance, rule, law
panniers, pair of baskets for balanced loads on a beast of burden
Papist, follower of Pope (Roman Catholic)
pastor, clergyman in charge of a church, minister
persecution, ill-treatment for beliefs held by the victim
pike, hand weapon consisting of a long wooden handle with a sharp
   steel or iron head
to pillage, to loot, steal, in time of war or violence
to prevail upon, to persuade successfully
providence, God's timely care
prow, front of a ship
quagmire, bog
quarter, (here) mercy
rapier, small sword
reader (of a church), one who reads prayers aloud
refined, fine, delicate
remiss, careless
to repel, to drive back
revenue, income
to revoke, to recall, withdraw
to rout, to put to disorderly flight
rustic, of the countryside
sailyard, long beam on which a sail is extended
scribe, writer, secretary
shrouds, ropes or wires supporting a mast
stint, period of work, shift
superfluity, more than is needed
swooning, fainting
symbolic, standing as a sign
thronged, crowded
tithe, tax of one-tenth payable to church
tocsin, alarm bell
toleration, freedom of religion
to transact, to do business
to traverse, to cross

trice (trise), instant
unstable, not reliable
viceroy, king's deputy, governor
vineyard, patch of ground where grape vines are grown
wake, track
weal, mark of lash on skin
yokel, uneducated country fellow

Acknowledgements

For permission to reproduce
illustrative material we are
grateful to the following:

Page

7	Rijksmuseum, Amsterdam
9	Rijksmuseum, Amsterdam
11	Bibliotheque Universitaire de Geneve
13	Radio Times Hulton Picture Library (R.T.H.P.L.)
14	Archives Photographiques, Paris
16	Mansell Collection
18	Giraudon
19	Archivo Mas, Prado, Madrid
21	Mary Evans Picture Library (M.E.P.L.)
23	M.E.P.L.
24	Lauros-Giraudon
27	M.E.P.L.
28	R.T.H.P.L.
29	M.E.P.L.
30/1	Musée Cantonal des Beaux-Arts, Lausanne
35	Archives Photographiques, Paris
36	Giraudon
37	Lauros-Giraudon
39	Mansell Collection
40	Giraudon
42	Bibliotheque Nationale, Paris
45	*both* Mansell Collection
46	Giraudon
47	Giraudon
48	Giraudon
49	Mansell Collection
50	Giraudon
51	H. Roger Viollet
52	H. Roger Viollet
55	M.E.P.L.
59	H. Roger Viollet
63	H. Roger Viollet
64	Giraudon
65	Giraudon
66	H. Roger Viollet
70	National Maritime Museum L, Greenwich
71	R.T.H.P.L.
76	Societe de l'Histoire du Protestantisme Français
77	*Left*
	right M.E.P.L.
80	North Devon Athenaeum
83	Reproduced by gracious permission of Her Majesty the Queen
87	*both* South African Embassy
88/9	Frick Collection, New York
91	Portal's Ltd
92	*left* Victoria and Albert Museum
92	*right* Christie, Manson and Woods Ltd
94	City Museum, Bristol
95	City Museum, Bristol
99	Bristol Public Libraries
100/1	Bristol Public Libraries